ROUTLEDGE LIBRARY EDITIONS: CURRICULUM

Volume 19

LEARNING ENVIRONMENTS FOR THE WHOLE CURRICULUM

LEARNING ENVIRONMENTS FOR THE WHOLE CURRICULUM

Edited by
DAVID HUSTLER, ETHEL MILROY AND
MIKE COCKETT

LONDON AND NEW YORK

First published in 1991 by Unwin Hyman

This edition first published in 2019
by Routledge
2 Park Square, Milton Park, Abingdon, Oxon OX14 4RN

and by Routledge
711 Third Avenue, New York, NY 10017

Routledge is an imprint of the Taylor & Francis Group, an informa business

British Library Cataloguing in Publication Data
A catalogue record for this book is available from the British Library

ISBN: 978-1-138-31956-1 (Set)
ISBN: 978-0-429-45387-8 (Set) (ebk)
ISBN: 978-1-138-31882-3 (Volume 19) (hbk)
ISBN: 978-0-429-45427-1 (Volume 19) (ebk)

Publisher's Note
The publisher has gone to great lengths to ensure the quality of this reprint but points out that some imperfections in the original copies may be apparent.

Disclaimer
The publisher has made every effort to trace copyright holders and would welcome correspondence from those they have been unable to trace.

Learning Environments for the Whole Curriculum

'It's not like normal lessons'

EDITED BY

**David Hustler, Ethel Milroy
and Mike Cockett**

London
UNWIN HYMAN
Boston   Sydney   Wellington

Published by the Academic Division of
Unwin Hyman Ltd
15/17 Broadwick Street, London W1V 1FP, UK

Unwin Hyman Inc.,
8 Winchester Place, Winchester, Mass. 01890, USA

Allen & Unwin (Australia) Ltd,
8 Napier Street, North Sydney, NSW 2060, Australia

Allen & Unwin (New Zealand) Ltd in association with the
Port Nicholson Press Ltd,
Compusales Building, 75 Ghuznee Street, Wellington 1, New Zealand

First published in 1991

British Library Cataloguing in Publication Data

Learning environments for the whole curriculum.
1. Education
I. Hustler, David   II. Milroy, Ethel   III. Cockett, Mike
370

ISBN 0-04-445400-7 pbk

Library of Congress Cataloging in Publication Data

Learning environments for the whole curriculum / edited by David
Hustler, Ethel Milroy, Mike Cockett.
    p.   cm.
Includes bibliographical references (p.).
ISBN 0-04-445400-7 (pbk.)
1. Education. Secondary—England—Manchester—Curricula.
2. Education. Secondary—Europe—Curricula.   I. Milroy,
Ethel.
II. Cockett, Michael.
LB1629.G7L35   1990
373.19'09—dc20   90–39840
                                                        CIP

Phototypeset in 10 on 11pt Baskerville by Input Typesetting Ltd, London
and printed in Great Britain by Billing and Sons Ltd, London and Worcester

Contents

PART II: PUPILS' LEARNING, TEACHERS' LEARNING AND THE QUALITY OF LEARNING

Notes on Contributors

Editors

David Hustler works at the School of Education, Manchester Polytechnic, where he has been particularly involved in collaborative research and school-based evaluation development with teachers. Ethel Milroy is a Senior Inspector with Manchester LEA. She was the Director of Manchester 'Alternative Curriculum Strategies' project. Mike Cockett co-ordinated Manchester's 'Alternative Curriculum Strategies' project and now directs Manchester's TVEI programme.

Kathy August, who was also heavily involved in the 'Alternative Curriculum Strategies' project and is now headteacher of a Manchester secondary school, was also very helpful in the initial editorial 'stages. All four members of this central team were involved in various ways in the European Transition Project.

Contributors

The book represents a period of close collaboration between a large number of contributors who work in differing sectors of the education system. From schools and colleges: Joan Bishop, Mike Moore, Gilly Walker, David Dickinson, Tom Cooley, Margaret Howard, Adrian Harrington, Jean-Pierre Kirkland, Finn Deloughry, Leslie Howard, Kristel Hartmann, Diane King, Sue Botcherby, Beryl Jackson, Brendan Agnew and Helen Strahan.

From Manchester's Advisory and Support Service: Lorna Borland, Mike Cockett, John Coghill, Ethel Milroy and Gerry Brown.

From the School of Education, Manchester Polytechnic: Gordon Baddeley, Alan Goodwin and David Hustler.

The thanks of all contributors must go to Liz Marsland and Barbara Ashcroft who typed, retyped, and typed again, the wide range of contributions to this book.

1

Introduction

This book is about some changes that took place in our secondary schools during the 1980s. These changes have led to teachers and pupils being involved in activities which will perhaps seem far removed not only from most readers' memories of their own schooling, but also from their notions of what goes on in schools currently. The changes represent a response from teachers and schools to the demands which were being voiced during the late 1970s and 1980s when our school system was under fire for its lack of adaptability to a changing economic and social context. Schools were criticized for being closed communities, isolated from the real world and dominated by an outdated examination structure, which gave success to very few while ensuring that most experienced failure. These demands came from parents, certainly from large numbers of employers, from teachers themselves, but interestingly enough also from government. As a consequence, a considerable amount of government funding went into projects designed to stimulate alternative approaches within our secondary schools and colleges.

Several of the contributors to this book were associated with the Alternative Curriculum Strategies project, which was based in Manchester. The sub-title of the book is, in fact, an off-the-cuff comment by one pupil about his early experience of this project. The full quote is 'It's not like normal lessons . . . you don't have to wag school any more'. For the uninitiated, 'wag' means 'bunk off', or 'truant'.

The Alternative Curriculum Strategies project has been described elsewhere (Cockett, 1986), but the principles informing this project have also been at the heart of attempts in many other parts of the country and elsewhere in Europe to bring our schools into the late twentieth century. The principles have been summarized (Hustler, Cassidy and Cuff, 1986), as follows:

- Pupils will respond better to a curriculum that is practical, experiential and which is clearly related to the 'real' world in which they live

- Learning strategies should be developed that promote co-operative rather than competitive learning
- The schools should be more open to their communities and the resources of the communities should be used in developing the alternative curriculum
- Pupils should be included in the decision-making process in relation to their own learning and this should be the heart of the new, more co-operative relationships between teachers and pupils
- New forms of assessment and accreditation should be developed which offer all pupils a chance of success

Certainly, many of these principles and commitments have a long educational history. The distinctive feature of the 1980s was the extent to which there were strong attempts to apply these principles. Manchester's Alternative Curriculum Strategies project was part of the National Lower Attaining Pupils project (LAPP), established in 1982 with a view to finding ways of transforming educational experiences for 'the bottom 40%' (Weston, 1988). The argument was that schooling was failing at least this percentage of its pupils, that school was not viewed as relevant, that it was boring, that it was not meeting the needs of almost half its pupils . . . and that many, over the age of 14, were already either voting with their feet or were present but not present.

Many of the principles associated with projects such as LAPP have also been increasingly apparent in a much more ambitious project: the Technical and Vocational Educational Initiative (TVEI). Whereas LAPP was funded by the Department of Education and Science (DES), TVEI was a drastic intervention into education from the Manpower Services Commission, now the Training Agency. The argument here was once again that schooling was failing to meet certain needs, but this time there was more emphasis on the failure of schools to meet the changing needs of society, and in particular the economy. Initially the TVEI project led to fierce debates about 'education' versus 'training', but as the project developed, and began to move from pilot stage towards extension to all schools, it increasingly lost the early narrow vocational image. There is already extensive literature about TVEI (Barton and Walker, 1986; Pollard, Purvis and Walford, 1988). The very first curriculum report in this book nicely illustrates many principles and features typical of TVEI developments in other Local Education Authorities (LEAs) and schools.

There is a temptation to suggest that the advent of the National Curriculum is 'year zero' in the education system with all that has gone before being prehistory and not directly relevant to present needs. The significance of this book is that it highlights issues which will return to haunt us unless the National Curriculum is implemented in a manner which takes account of the needs, the good practice and the variety of learning environments described here. The argument is that the alternative forms of schooling described in the book are an essential part of the curriculum experience for all pupils. It is argued by some that aspects of current moves to implement the National Curriculum, and in particular its associated assessment and testing programme, may well squeeze such alternatives out of school life (Broadfoot, 1988). However, the materials in this book are presented to help schools to consider ways of weaving such approaches into their National Curriculum frameworks. As the DES document on the National Curriculum, *From Policy to Practice* notes:

TVEI criteria reflect the statutory requirements to teach all foundation subjects, whilst allowing for the particular emphases of TVEI. The stimulus given by TVEI to thinking about curriculum organisation and delivery should stand schools in good stead in planning for the introduction of the new statutory requirements.

(DES, 1989 4.13).

The major part of this book consists of short curriculum reports by teachers regarding their attempts to improve the learning opportunities and experiences of the pupils with whom they work. The focus is very much on developments in schooling from the age of 14 upwards and many, but by no means all, of the reports involved pupils who were by this age somewhat disenchanted with their schools and who might be regarded as failures. Another way of putting this is that our school system is failing these pupils. This is certainly the viewpoint that the contributors to this book take. The teachers' reports vary tremendously in style, but this variety adds, we believe, to the strength of the book. The organizing editors were keen to allow teachers to speak for themselves and not to feel constrained by too uniform a format or by the feeling that their words would be transformed for the purposes of publication. In fact the very process of producing the book was designed as a staff development exercise for many of the contributors, including teachers, educational advisers and inspectors, project co-ordinators and polytechnic lecturers involved in teacher education. The strong commitment

of all was to the value of written accounts of our practice and
our beliefs, as a major device for jointly learning more about
schooling and our approaches to it. There is no doubt that for
the contributors it has indeed been a learning experience, and
we hope that the same will be true for readers of this book.

The decision was made at an early stage to produce a book
aimed at a general and diverse audience. With this in mind, we
have attempted to avoid extensive theorizing and have regarded
it as more important to provide accounts of school activities
about which readers can form their own judgements. We have
also deliberately attempted to minimize references to the body
of extensive literature which is available on many of the topics
to which we refer. We imagine that many parents might be
interested in the book, as might those who are thinking about,
or in the process of entering, teaching as a career. For those with
a new interest in what is happening in our schools, the teachers'
reports may be surprising. They do not fit easily with dominant
notions of what schooling is like. They may seem a long way
removed from the reader's memories of his or her own life at
school; memories perhaps of teachers writing on blackboards in
front of pupils seated in rows of desks, memories of the sorts of
relationships they had with their teachers, memories of the
choices they were allowed and what approaches to learning were
encouraged. One purpose of this book is simply to indicate some
of the changes that took place, for some pupils in some schools,
during the 1980s. There is certainly no intention of pretending
that the reports presented here paint a good picture of what is
happening most of the time in our schools. What is being suggested is that in many of our schools, developments similar to
those described in some of these reports are emerging.

The materials in this book should be of interest to those teachers who are themselves attempting to devise innovative strategies
within their own schools and classrooms, and who share to some
extent the principles outlined above. It might even be that the
book will be read by those with real decision-making powers
about our education system. To all these people, the question
we would wish to pose is to what extent the opportunity can
be taken to strengthen these alternative approaches. They will
certainly have to be fought for if schools focus overmuch on too
narrow a subject-based implementation of statutory requirements. It is crucial to recognize that there is only one real
programme of study, not discrete pieces: that programme is the
whole curriculum into which the special core and foundation

subjects are planned elements but never the totality, and that those core and foundation subjects also have to work in harmony.

Structure of the book

Part I, the lengthiest and most important section, consists of curriculum reports written by teachers. It is divided into three chapters, and each curriculum report has a brief editorial introduction. The chapters correspond roughly to three senses in which the curriculum reports involve departures from 'normal school'. The first chapter includes reports of changes within classrooms and specific subject areas. There is, in some of these studies, an emphasis on the importance of changing the actual layout of classrooms – the physical environment for learning. We also felt it was important to include reports in core subject areas and the two represented here are English and mathematics. For many readers, these classrooms will not seem like 'normal' classrooms, nor will it seem like 'normal' maths or 'normal' English.

The second chapter in Part I focuses on the uses that are made of settings outside the school. 'Normal' schooling for many means entering the school gates at about 8.45 a.m. and leaving at 4 p.m. Many teachers are convinced that schooling can only connect powerfully with the 'real' world if it embraces it to some extent, and displays this through teachers and pupils moving beyond the boundaries of the school.

The third chapter has as its unifying theme some extended ways in which school time and space within the school have undergone changes. The concern of some reports here is with moving away from complete domination by the 'normal' school timetable of 40 minute slots for this subject or that subject, and towards giving pupils some say in how they organize their time and space. Out of school settings are also the focus for some of these reports, though in this section the studies concern themselves particularly with the inter-relationship between work in the school and out of the school.

Some of the curriculum reports come from other parts of Europe. Earlier we noted that the curriculum reports are associated with many of the principles built into projects such as TVEI. In fact, these principles are also explicit within the European Community's programme 'Transition from School to Adult and Working Life'. This programme has managed to involve teachers across Europe in working collaboratively on innovative learning environments.

Part II consists of four brief 'issues' chapters. They represent four perspectives on the curriculum reports; the first of these, Chapter 5, considers the shared general principles which seem to inform contributors' views about teaching and learning. Some readers might find it useful to read this chapter earlier rather than later.

Chapter 6 considers ways in which the teachers themselves have been learning, and moves on to discuss approaches to staff development. Whatever readers may make of many of the approaches illustrated in the curriculum reports, there is little doubt in our minds that the commitment on the part of the writers, their capacity to work hard, their concern for pupils and enthusiasm for education, will be apparent again and again. There is little here to suggest that teachers are unwilling to change their practices or are uninterested in attempting to improve the life chances of the pupils with whom they work. Of course, we are not suggesting that all teachers display these qualities, what we are saying is that many do. We are also suggesting that these capacities are worth backing and that they are one of the strongest resources which the education system has. The key feature which these studies point to is that when teachers are given the backing, the opportunity and some freedom to innovate, they can be a most powerful force for change.

In several ways, many of these curriculum reports have much in common with a movement within education known as action research (Carr and Kemmis, 1986; Hustler, Cassidy and Cuff, 1986; McNiff, 1988). The starting point for many of the reports published here is a commitment to narrow the gap between aspirations for one's teaching and its reality. Initially, there is often some concern about how the needs of a particular group of pupils do not seem to be being met, or a desire to attempt to implement certain principles. A recurring feature of the reports is that teachers are attempting to learn more about what does or does not work, as regards improving practice, through trying out different strategies.

There are, of course, aspects of the reports which could be challenged and certainly those with commitments to action research would find grounds on which to criticize the work reported here. Several readers would want clearer evidence relating to changes and the consequence of changes, many would want less eulogy and more rigour, perhaps slightly less 'action' and a lot more 'research'. The eulogy is important, however, because amongst other things it points to the motivational impact upon teachers of their experience as reported in the curriculum reports.

Chapter 6 pursues some of these issues as well as discussing some of the more general changes in approaches to staff development over the last few years. What is worth noting is the strong parallel, in terms of educational principles, between Chapter 5 as regards what should inform learning for pupils, and Chapter 6 regarding what should inform learning for teachers.

Chapter 7 pursues matters which relate to the assessment of learning experiences and learning outcomes. The teachers writing the curriculum reports frequently refer to what they take to be the major learning outcomes for their pupils. These vary, of course, according to the particular area or activity, but there does tend to be a set of themes which cut across almost all the reports, whether the report focuses on design education, English literature, mathematics or pottery. The themes are concerned with taking responsibility for one's own learning, recognizing one's own abilities, learning to work with others, acquiring flexibility and the ability to respond to new situations, learning about your own and others' personal qualities, and learning that you can learn in school.

In the early 1980s there was much talk of the need for an 'education for life' and these qualities were often said to be precisely what schooling was not able to deliver, but what society needed and young people needed as they moved into further training and employment. These curriculum reports indicate some of the ways in which teachers have been responding to these criticisms. One major shared feature has been the view that pupils need to be much more involved in their schooling and become more active participants in the learning process rather than passive bystanders. It is hardly surprising, given this, that most of the reports place great store on the need to motivate pupils. It is also worth bearing in mind that many of the teachers were working with pupils who did not think much of school. High motivation and effective learning are viewed in many of the reports as being strongly interrelated. We return to some of the ironies associated with this in Chapter 8. Readers will make their own judgements regarding the quality and nature of the learning experiences described in the reports. What is clear, however, is that as teachers recognized the need to bring about changes in school life so as to incorporate the above themes into pupils' learning experiences, they also recognized the need to develop different forms of assessment and accreditation.

(Chapter 7 also discusses some of the major dilemmas built into assessment, particularly as the implementation of the National Curriculum and its associated testing programme gathers pace.)

The topic discussed in Chapter 8, is rather different. This chapter attempts to describe some of the pupils' own viewpoints and judgements about being involved in schooling which did not seem like 'normal school'. Perhaps we should make explicit the fact that we have deliberately not attempted to define 'normal school'. For most of our readers, the connotations of this will be perfectly obvious, any definition we would have proposed would have been easily bettered by many of the comments made by the pupils in this chapter. Changing the classroom environment, breaking down some of the barriers between school and out of school, changing the basic form of the school timetable, can lead to real challenges to our common sense assumptions regarding what constitutes a legitimate learning experience. At the same time, recalling the debates and demands over the last ten years, the basic point is precisely that schools do need to change drastically, that we do need to revise our ideas as to what shape schooling should take so as to be more responsive to both the needs of most of our pupils and the needs of a changing economic environment. The issue confronting us now is how the changes illustrated by these curriculum reports can help schools to continue to change within the context of implementing the National Curriculum. There is no doubt that the pupils' views as represented in Chapter 8 would seem to demand such elements as part of school life.

The four 'issues' chapters provide particular ways of reconsidering the material in terms of pupils learning, teachers learning, assessment, and pupils' judgements. This particular selection of issues is not arbitrary, but there are clearly many other major issues raised by the curriculum reports. In our concluding comments, we discuss some of these and our reasons for not addressing them in depth here. It may be useful to know that the 'issues' chapters were written after the curriculum reports, and after considerable discussion with many of the teachers who wrote the reports.

Finally, we should make one thing very clear. We do not hold up all of the reports in this book as shining examples of good practice. Many of them can be criticized in a variety of ways, and we are sure that our readers will not find themselves short of resources here. They do, however, represent examples of attempts to build new learning experiences into school life, attempts which, to a greater or lesser degree, reflect the principles outlined above and which are developed further in Chapter 5. For many of the teachers involved, the curriculum reports are in fact very early attempts which have by now been further refined. We regard the reports as a resource for imaginative whole curriculum planning. It is our view that the National Curriculum requirements must be viewed, not so much as a constraint, but rather as an opportunity to develop coherent strategies relating curriculum content, learning environments and teaching and learning approaches. We would argue, and argue very strongly, that our schools need the sorts of approaches illustrated by these curriculum reports. Our schools need them, because our young people need them if they are to develop the skills, understanding, confidence and self-esteem to make their way within, and contribute powerfully to, a changing society, a society which, we must remember, is drastically different from that which 'normal' schooling was designed to serve.

PART I

Teachers' Curriculum Reports

2

Changing Settings within the School

A new learning environment for business and information studies

JOAN BISHOP, MIKE MOORE and GILLY WALKER

The figures in this chapter (Figs. 2.1 and 2.2) illustrate a quite dramatic shift from so-called 'normal' classrooms. In fact, such environments are now much more common in our secondary schools than some may imagine, and many of these developments are associated with the TVEI project and its extension. Curricular areas such as business studies have received high priority within this project and the reader will note many of the parallels between this classroom environment and business settings. For the authors of the chapter, however, it is the changes in learning styles and learning opportunities which receive the most attention. The implication is that changes to the nature of the physical setting are strongly associated with the learning experiences of both students and staff.

In May 1986 Salford's bid to be involved in the Technical and Vocational Education Initiative (TVEI), funded by the Manpower Services Commission, was accepted and five schools then had to develop courses for fourth- and fifth-year pupils starting in September. There was little time.

It was agreed that a small committee consisting of a deputy headteacher, and the heads of business studies and computer education would look at business studies and information technology courses. They quickly set about the task – making visits to other schools and colleges, collecting information from far and near, scouring GCSE syllabuses and scrutinizing the examinations offered by other regional and national examining boards.

It was finally decided that the school would offer business and information studies (in a version known to some as the 'Hampshire Scheme'), a double option designed to integrate the twin themes of 'business' and 'information studies'. The course is taught as an entity, not as two subjects. In assessment, the two components are separated and two GCSE examination certificates are awarded, one for business studies and one for information studies. Team teaching is normal and the information technology theme is used as a tool for the development and enhancement of the business theme. The course is student-centred with a wide range of learning assignments covering the learning objectives and systematically developing the social and interpersonal skills by way of profiles. The teacher thus becomes a facilitator and adviser rather than the director of all learning. This has meant massive relearning for the teacher but we have found it a rewarding and interesting experience which has affected the way in which we teach other classes.

Three rooms were allocated for the course. The computer room had already been refurbished and contained fifteen BBC 32K computers and five Master computers. The typing room was stripped, electric points were fitted round the room and Visual Display Unit tables which could be linked together to form interesting shapes were installed. Shelving units, white board, overhead projectors and filing cabinets were bought. The windows were curtained, new lights were fitted, the floor was carpeted and, coincidentally, during the holiday the school was decorated. Ten Amstrad PCW 8256 computers and ten electronic typewriters were installed. New swivel chairs completed the scene. The room was renamed 'business education'. The adjacent maths room was converted to a 'business activity' room with movable furniture, screens, reception area, small kitchen area, bookcases for resource material, telephone training system, lateral filing and a large photocopier. Plants and flowers are grouped in all rooms and each room has a stockroom (see Figs. 2.1 and 2.2). The refurbishing has proved to be most successful and has been adopted by the LEA as a model for the furnishing of other schools.

Radical changes have taken place in teaching and learning experiences for both pupils and staff to the advantage of both. Pupils have been encouraged to attempt to solve problems without waiting for teacher direction. They tend to have more individual attention and help and have shown an increase in maturity and the ability to exercise initiative in new and challenging situations. Their self-confidence, self-reliance and expertise have been enhanced. The competence of the pupils has often proved invaluable and they are always willing to share knowledge with staff or with fellow pupils. They can converse easily with the increasing number of visitors and will give verbal reports and explanations of their work. They are keen to take on technology and to attempt new areas. They often work on when school

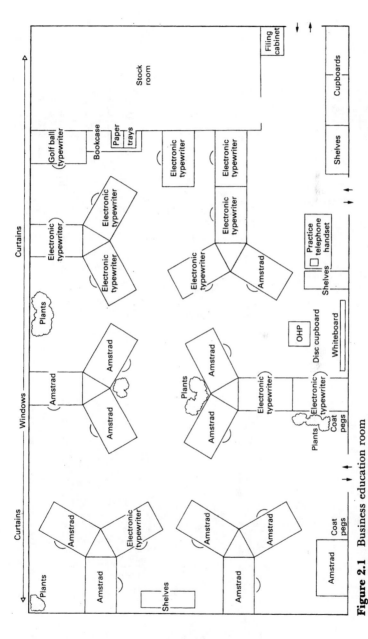

Figure 2.1 Business education room

Note: Amstrad PCWs and electronic typewriters are not 'fixed' in these positions. They can be used in the business activity room or in the computer room – and often are.

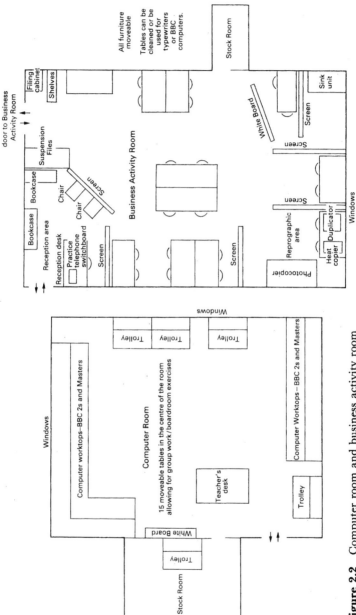

Figure 2.2 Computer room and business activity room

finishes and we have to keep an 'overtime book' to record this extra work. Video recordings, tape recordings and photographs have been included in their work. They tend to be more self-critical and more eager to help each other. Working as part of a team is an integral part of the course work with groups of pupils co-operating and compromising in order to complete assignments. Group leaders have sometimes emerged naturally and at other times have developed through the necessity for some kind of 'ruling vote'.

Decision making has improved in almost all pupils as a result of being responsible for their own progress rather than waiting for the teacher to direct them. We gave up buying sets of books – much of our resource material is now centred on the departmental library to which we are constantly adding.

Pupils and staff enjoy working together. The atmosphere is friendly, relaxed and purposeful and our enthusiasm remains undimmed.

The work experience during the fourth year was generally of great value to them and they still talk about it, six months later. They now realize the need to be more disciplined in their approach to work and responsible in their attitudes – arriving on time, having the right equipment, attending regularly. They have commented on the similarity of work they have done in school and that which they experienced while working in industry.

Residential experience was included for all pupils in their fourth year and was based on outdoor pursuits, although much of the emphasis was on leadership and responsibility. Activities such as rock climbing and potholing were included to challenge pupils and, it is hoped, to make them more aware of their own personal qualities – perseverance, helpfulness, reliability, trustworthiness. Teachers had to develop skills for debriefing after activities and counselling of pupils in order to make them more aware of what they had achieved and experienced.

The staff too, have changed. They are more relaxed in the new role they have adopted and less authoritarian in their approach to children. The commitment and enthusiasm of the staff involved seemed to grow from day to day. We moved out of our own 'boxes' and became a team which moved freely from business studies to computer education and information technology with reasonable ease. Respect for the expertise of our colleagues grew and was freely available when called upon. We teach as a team which of course requires a great deal of co-operation between the staff involved – planning, communicating, preparing, reviewing and assessing. Of course, three 'experts' in the classroom can be a problem in itself, so if the team approach is to work, staff must be prepared to allow others 'the floor' and yet not abuse the situation by opting out of responsibilities. It is also an opportunity for staff to gain experience in subject areas other than their own and to observe colleagues' practices and methods.

Being constantly observed by your colleagues can be a little daunting at first, although it does tend to sharpen up your presentation. We were fortunate to have attractive teaching areas which allowed flexibility of group sizes and activities. The varying areas of knowledge and experience of the staff have been used to the full and they have all been fully committed to the course and to the changes needed in teaching method and organization. This has been achieved only after full and lengthy discussions and by a willingness on their part to change, compromise, adapt, relearn and experiment. A strong team has been built and maintained and we believe that this has created a realistic atmosphere on the course. When our pupils go out to work they are far more likely to be working as members of teams and to have more than one person to whom they can turn for help and guidance.

The assessment of pupils' work falls within two areas: formal assessment by objectively assessed assignments and informal, subjective assessment by the teacher. Assessed assignments take the form of mini case studies on production, business data management, marketing and business decision making. A pupil must also select four pieces of work for assessment of a portfolio.

Schools mark the assignments and then join a consensus moderation group for moderation. Forty per cent of the final marks in each subject are given to course work. The other 60 per cent is awarded for the final case study which is completed during the final three weeks of the course. Differentiated papers are available at this stage allowing students to be assessed within their own ability range.

In addition pupils have been entered for Royal Society of Arts core text processing and various grades of typewriting examinations offered by North West Regional Advisory Council for Further Education. We hope to extend the range of qualifications which can be achieved according to the individual needs and readiness of our pupils.

We have realized that there is a need for in-service training, particularly in view of rapidly changing technology and the inevitable changes in the course work as pupils gain experience lower down the school.

Locally based assignments are to be written and we have become aware of the need for cross-curricular developments for other staff who have become involved, not just in the course work but in the use of the word processors. Several departments have now purchased word processors for their own use.

We would welcome an input on the Technical and Vocational Education Initiative Control Technology course being offered in school but so far this has not been possible because of timetabling difficulties. We are aware of the need for an introduction to elements of this type of course in the first three years of secondary education.

We have enjoyed the contacts with schools outside our own Local Education Authority during consensus moderation meetings, and we have gained much from the mutual co-operation which has developed. We hope that some in-service training across LEA boundaries may be possible. We have been pleased with the balance of the sexes in the course and with the equal opportunities which it has engendered. We are delighted that pupils will now select for themselves the machinery they need to complete any task using information technology as a tool.

The environment we have created seems to have proved successful and both pupils and staff are happy with the conditions under which they work.

Creating an appropriate environment for design education

DAVID DICKINSON

The implicit arguments in the business studies contribution are pursued in much more detail here. As the author notes: 'We have attempted to provide for the pupils an environment in which they can actively develop "designerly thinking" . . . '.

Issues such as how a room is named, the colour scheme and the presence of carpets, are discussed in terms of their impact on students' learning experiences. It is perhaps in areas such as design education, or craft and design technology, that some of the messages conveyed by the learning environment are most obvious and have received most discussion. The author notes, for example, the impact on girls of traditional school workshops. The section of this case study should perhaps lead us to reconsider the messages conveyed by the learning environments traditionally associated with other curricular areas.

I was fortunate in that when I became involved with the design department on which this case study focuses, very little already existed. The school had been established as the result of an amalgamation between two smaller schools, neither of which had any firmly established ethos of design education. A city-centre site had been purchased to house the new school, on the doorstep of the university, polytechnic and the city's main museums and galleries. This proximity to the centre was later to enable the pupils to experience a wide range of learning environments, and to use considerable resources for their research, all within the timespan of a normal double lesson.

Before discussing the learning environment, and how the pupils and staff use it in the course of design-related activities, it is important that certain curriculum considerations are outlined briefly, so that the reader can gauge the appropriateness of the environment in meeting those needs, and form a mental image of design education as we perceive it.

The whole area of design education has been widely interpreted, there being a range of often disparate perceptions not only at school level but even within the policy-making bodies of the Schools Examination Council and the government. In fact, at the time of writing this case study, many of those involved in design education nationally have suspended curriculum work, awaiting a clear definition from the secretary of state, as a part of the National Curriculum plan.

The role of design education as we see it, is to enable pupils to develop an appropriate language, and the relevant cognitive and physical skills, to explore critically and to contribute to the built or made environment. With that aim in mind, the course that we offer to the pupils is process rather than content based.

The activities are structured to encourage pupils to think and know in what has come to be known as a 'designerly way'. 'Designerly ways of knowing', a term originated by the Royal College of Art, can be taken in this instance to include: '[the ability] of the designer to effect a translation from individual, organizational and social needs to physical artifacts.'

We have attempted to provide an environment for the pupils in which they can actively develop designerly thinking, as well as such skills as critical awareness; an understanding of what makes artifacts or ideas useful, attractive, possible or indeed otherwise. They are then given the opportunity to produce the resulting models or working artifacts to a high standard.

The pupils are then encouraged to evaluate their own outcomes, and the work of their classmates to see how well their realizations satisfy their own goals.

We try to ensure that these goals are not presented to the students routinely or arbitrarily by teacher or textbook: instead they result from an individual, guided investigation into core issues relating to such matters as the learner's image or self in society and his or her relationship with others, ways of taking or directing action and so on.

This type of teaching strategy requires a very different learning environment from that normally associated with subjects in the craft design and technology genre and within the limitations of the existing architecture, these have been created but not without a few difficulties that are worth outlining.

The rooms selected for the design department consisted of two blocks: a pair of multi-role studios for the younger pupils, and one room each for the 'product design', 'design communication' and 'design technology' studios, each block being serviced by two preparation areas. It may sound pretentious to call these rooms studios, but the more common expression, 'workshop', did nothing to convey to the youngsters or indeed the staff and parents, the range of activities from which the proposed curriculum would allow them to choose.

Initially I was given a very light teaching commitment to enable me to 'expedite matters' as it was quaintly put, and without training I was placed in the role of purchaser, finance administrator, progress chaser and liaison officer, but with an interesting twist. Because my status was that of teacher, whenever I was passed from one local government department to the next by some well-intentioned agent, this invariably involved climbing a hierarchical ladder. Every so often I would speak to someone who was not accustomed to being addressed by a mere teacher and the headteacher was asked to warn off the young upstart.

On another occasion I discovered that certain large equipment suppliers offer a free planning service to Local Education Authorities, in much the same way as do fitted kitchen firms to the householder. In my experience they tend to be partisan in their view of what other facilities might be required and hold a limited understanding of, or cavalier disregard for, the space needed by the children themselves.

The design communication studio was to be carpeted. This was so as not only to reduce noise, but also an attempt to foster a professional attitude to what is after all a serious and demanding activity. The recently retired director of the innovative Stantonbury Campus in Milton Keynes, Geoff Cooksey, claimed that his most successful curriculum initiative ever was in having the whole school carpeted.

It has long been understood that the dirty, factory-like environment of the traditional school workshops does little to interest girls, and far less in enticing them when it comes to option time. Although I had no intention of adding heavy engineering or machining elements to enable all pupils to achieve an appropriately professional standard of finish to make outcomes of rigid and resistive materials, a number of machines were going to be essential. My instinct was to select brightly coloured, unintimidating machines on which controls, guards and other features were uncomplicated and visually attractive. Much to the amusement of colleagues in other schools, and in particular the machine tool suppliers, I made these my selection criteria from the outset. I have been in no way dissatisfied with the choices that I made, apart from the fact that one or two machines that we needed only came in sage green and primer grey. Colour too was an important consideration when it came to the walls of the rooms, but this was a battle that I had little chance of winning, the architects having firm opinions about the colours that 'workshops' are painted.

As for the benches in these studios, I once again opted for flexibility, selecting large, general purpose workbenches with the added bonus of two bogey wheels and a jacking point. The idea is that when the bench is in use, the wheels, situated at one end of the frame, are just touching the floor but bearing no weight. When a small, wheeled jack is positioned under the other end, the weight is taken off the legs onto the wheels, allowing the bench to be moved easily around the studio, creating space for role play, large projects and so forth.

Unfortunately, the project for the refurbishment of the whole campus ran into financial difficulties and the design suite, ostensibly because it was going to cost the most, suffered the most cuts. The new benches, (bogey wheels and all), some of the new machinery, the carpet for the communication studio, and a vast array of tools and equipment were struck from the schedules, the idea being to use the facilities that were on the stock books at the other site. On the stock books they might have been, but their usability, appropriateness or availability was another matter. There were a number of dilapidated woodwork benches upon which abused vices hung in varying states of decline, and three vast traditional metalwork benches with vices that had been handpainted in purple, turquoise and red, apparently before the preceding coats had dried. If anything had the potential to demonstrate to pupils that the quality of their working environment had little importance, it was those benches. I did win a little ground back from the treasury though, and the benches have since been refurbished. As for the vices, they have been stripped down and painted in primary yellow.

The repainting of equipment in school studios and workshops is quite a common practice but often this is done with no colour scheme in mind, with old paint and little care, the results often making matters worse than they were before. A professional job is essential if the right attitudes about the built environment are to be established with our pupils. The use of bright colours is, as I mentioned previously, supportive of an appropriate hidden curriculum, but at the school in question they have a special significance. The school has facilities for mainstreaming blind and visually impaired pupils and as any teacher of practical subjects is aware, because vices protrude from a bench, preoccupied pupils tend to walk into them. This type of minor accident has not yet occurred, probably due to the conspicuous colour.

The working environments that the pupils are encouraged to utilize, are not limited to the design studio, the school or indeed the community. Sometimes, working within the community can actually be limiting because of its size and the inaccessibility of necessary information and this is where we have found modelling and simulation to be invaluable. Much of designing involves decision-making and we have found from experience that when pupils are asked to become involved in planning projects concerning the community, they find it difficult to get the necessary information regardless of how helpful the local council officers are.

We have found the answer to be a large model town, clearly laid out with streets of houses, blocks of industry, schools and so forth. Use of architectural models (cars, people, trees and such) all contribute to the verisimilitude of this miniature environment. Scaled maps of the area, showing house numbers, road plans and so on, and a comprehensive data base giving the people living in each house, their status and occupation, are available for the pupils so that they can select only that information that they require for their particular research. The use of an architect's periscope to get a 'worm's eye' view of the model, has been particularly useful in assisting pupils who have difficulty in transferring ideas from two to three dimensions and back. One particular project for the third-year course involves teams of five pupils acting in the role of planning teams who

have been granted a sum of money to establish a small leisure
park for children of an age group of their choice. By accessing
the information on the data base and by consulting various sheets
containing such information as, for example, which trees have
conservation orders or which land has been selected for future
building projects, they can narrow down an available plot of
land for their work. When they have all the necessary information
to enable them to start, the pupils can then start to design and
model their selected site in a larger scale (the village is on a
scale of 1:25 to suit the flexible model people, again professional
architect models, that we have obtained to help them to relate
to the other difficult concept of scaling).

The criticism of a project such as this could be that the whole
thing is just a little too clean, an oversimplification of real life.
To get round this problem a number of 'wild cards' have been
prepared, for example letters from residents' pressure groups,
information concerning underground workings, sites of historic
importance which require immediate attention (usually in the
form of a word-processed letter), or some other issue which could
involve a major compromise. Wild cards, as well as enriching
the project with relevant social and political issues at an appropriate level, offer an excellent strategy for stretching the brightest
pupil and injecting a flagging pupil with new motivation.

As well as an exhibition of the work at the end of the course,
the penultimate session takes place in the drama studio with a
drama group, also third years, who act out the role of residents
who live at specific houses so that they too can relate to the
simulated environment. Each planning group then takes it in
turn to present their design proposal and model, and depending
upon the role character that the residents have developed in
previous drama lessons, they respond to the proposals as individuals, favourably or otherwise. At the end of each meeting the
residents are encouraged to cast a vote as to which proposal they
would like for their town, giving the planners a hard evaluation
of their work. The whole session is recorded on video for use in
the final session which is used for teacher and pupil evaluation
and profile negotiation.

The success of this simulated environment has been apparent
not just from the obvious enjoyment and involvement that boys
and girls alike have demonstrated, but also from the way in
which subsequent independent work has been approached, meth-
odically, more rigorously and indeed, more professionally.

The pottery development

TOM COOLEY

This report draws on several of the features of the first two curriculum reports, harnessed in this case to the running of a small pottery business within the school and with a strong emphasis on a quality product. School-based businesses, large and small, are now very much part of the educational scene and have led to fierce discussion as to their merits. This particular report makes much of the quality control process and its links to market research, costing and advertising elements. At the same time, the teacher involved points strongly to how the pottery experience could be seen to allow achievement of a kind not experienced in 'normal' classrooms, and one which promotes a wide range of learning outcomes.

This section discusses running a small scale pottery business, the products of which are of sufficiently professional standards to be marketed and sold by the pupils themselves. The operation works very much as a co-operative venture. The work is accredited by the Northern Examination Association unit credit system. There are two units which have been written and validated, to cover the processes and learning outcomes involved. The first unit is slipcast ceramics and to gain accreditation each student must make and finish one item of pottery using what is known as the slipcasting technique. The student has to be aware of quality control at each stage of the process, which entails checking for cracks and other faults. The pottery has to compare with factory made items. The second unit allied to the course is entitled 'Marketing and Selling: an Introduction'. This is a business and cross-curricular unit. The description of the unit is as follows:

The student will research a market in order to see whether or not a particular product will sell in the market. S/he will then survey the market in order to determine the appropriate cost for the product. The students then produce the advertising and sell the product, keeping accounts of sales.

This course uses a variety of different learning environments. The production side takes place in a pottery room which is also a general art room with a lot of visual stimulus; things like pot plants, pupils' work, batik and handmade pottery, make for a relaxed non-rigid environment. The atmosphere in the room is informal, with pupils working co-operatively through the production stages. There are no desks as such, pupils work around groups of tables either individually or together, depending on the tasks in hand.

Quality control is a high priority, emphasized throughout the production stages. It is extremely important to pupil esteem and personal satisfaction that the finished product is of high quality. A second rate final product does nothing to enhance motivation, whereas a quality finished product is an object of personal pride.

The learning environment for the research and costing is our local area, the City of Manchester, and costing surveys are done via shop surveys. The students are also encouraged to discuss the course and costing with their parents at home.

Personal and social education lessons take place prior to any sale of goods. Lessons on how to deal with customers, setting out the stall and so on are tackled prior to any sale. There is also some work on basic book-keeping. The pupils produce posters and arrange for advertising to be displayed. Due to limited production facilities, most of the selling goes on within the school at parent association functions such as Christmas and summer fairs. A lot of goods have also been sold to teachers, parents and friends. The product range we have is quite extensive and includes: teapots, mugs, lamp bases, cheese dishes, storage containers, various vases, plates and ornaments. Most of our moulds are bought from Stoke-on-Trent.

An essential part of the course and a vital learning environment are visits to working potteries. These are financed from profits and the two we use are Hornsea Pottery, Lancaster, and Gladstone Pottery Museum, Stoke.

On these visits the pupils see the working of a commercial pottery and appreciate that there are a lot of similarities with their own operation. Of course the most important aim of the day is that it should be exciting and fun. Any profits remaining after the visits are put back into the business.

The course was established in the school as part of the Alternative Curriculum Strategies project (ACS). ACS was organized in the city to provide a more meaningful and relevant curriculum for the so-called 'lower attaining pupils'. Blackley Pottery involves active experiential learning, giving the young people a series of different learning experiences. For these reasons we decided to include this course on the ACS timetable.

The course provides a wide range of learning experiences for both the teacher and the pupils involved. The whole of the activity is person-centred. For the pupils involved in this type of co-operative unit, they have to first learn to work together. The group tasks require a mature and co-operative attitude, working for the good of the team as opposed to being selfish and working on individual projects. This course enables the teacher to work with the youngsters in a more adult fashion, high expectations and high quality goods are built into the course. In fact the staff insist upon a high standard from the outset in terms of finished products and the production process. There are several other pottery and practical projects introduced into the course to maintain interest and variety. The staff find that because of the relaxed informal nature of the course the 'hidden curriculum' of interpersonal skills is a very important element of the course. The pupils learn new skills, they also gain a lot of technical knowledge and terminology. Social and personal skills are also enhanced via the selling and marketing aspects of the pottery.

Of course, this type of innovation requires heavy initial capital investment. At my school, we had to purchase a 'blunger', a liquid clay machine which cost approximately £500. There were already kilns on site. Technical assistance is also vital for activities such as material preparation, packing and firing of kilns. Teachers working on a small scale could economize by purchasing a cheaper, smaller mixer and by buying premixed liquid clay.

One major problem encountered by the teacher was that the children found it very difficult to use coloured glazing techniques, the final product became shabby in appearance. To overcome this problem we have adopted a white bodied clay with a clear glaze for all our products. The clear product decorated with bought-in transfers has proved to be far superior.

Further developments are envisaged, whereby pupils could make their own plastic moulds, and two-piece moulds made from found objects. A variety of decorative techniques – slip trailing into the moulds and splattering of oxides onto the bisque ware have already been tried, but it is hoped that pupils will eventually design and make their own screenprinted transfers. The next step is to purchase a spray booth and spraying equipment; funds permitting.

Other problems we have come up against include handling of the fragile produce and plaster moulds. The pupils tend to be clumsy at first and breakages do occur. Production skills have to be learnt and some of the initial skills can be repetitive, it is therefore good advice to have a few stages on the go at once to avoid boredom. Pride in the finished product can often overcome the initial frustration. The setup in school is modelled upon industrial methods used in the slipcast industry. Teachers need to fact find in advance to learn about setting up a casting table, mould emptying and so on, and to see how to adapt industrial methods to a school environment.

Given adequate preparation and resources, slipcast pottery can provide a stimulating and challenging learning environment for young people, and with a bit of luck it may also make some money for the school, and perhaps uncover a few budding entrepreneurs.

Multi-skills bases

ACS STAFF

Reading and writing can be accomplished at desks, but more practical activities are difficult. A variety of learning outcomes is to some extent determined by the provision of alternative resources. Space organized to provide a good primary learning base allows this to occur. Storage space, a sink, wet and dry areas, word processors or typewriters, paint and practical equipment, shift and extend the possibilities.

The multi-skills work base embodies these kinds of activities. A teacher could negotiate learning targets and varied outcomes without major timetable shifts. Different pupils could share parts of a major enterprise with resources to hand, spontaneous needs can be met. The creativity of the moment can be realized without the need to put a check on development until plans for specialist rooms can be realized. Restless students can shift their activity with the minimum of disruption.

Desks speak of 'normal' classrooms, and reading and writing are real work. So work comes to be reappraised. 'Before you just sat with a pen and wrote . . . that's all you ever do', said one student. Students come to recognize the value of practical experience, it is more informative. 'You learn more doing it than just writing about it'. Is it school still? It is recognized as school but different. 'If I was in school I wouldn't have done the work; on the course there is more opportunity to do what you'd like in lessons. It's not normally like stuck at a desk in the classrooms.' The increasing student ownership allows a reappraisal of school as it is.

The learning space takes on other characteristics. It is safe, and a place of belonging. The base may be decorated with a mural because 'it's ours'. Familial and domestic atmospheres are strengthened. Relationships still have to be managed, and may be more complex. If extended time is spent with a group there is no possibility of walking away from difficulty. Heavy control disappears. The sense of ownership is demonstrated in what may seem very trivial ways: 'You're allowed to move about. You can get up and about if you feel like it' . . . 'You can make yourself a drink when you feel like it.'

The creation of a multi-skills base in the Alternative Curriculum

Strategies project schools was a deliberate attempt to move away from the traditional classrooms with pupils' desks and chairs arranged in rows, facing a teacher's desk with a blackboard behind it. When people are organized in this way, with this type of furniture, the range of activities possible is generally limited to reading and writing. Anything which could be described as active learning is almost impossible in such a physically restricted space.

The 'multi-skills base' aimed, then, at providing a flexible, active learning environment. As the bases began to develop it became clear that they mirrored good classrooms in primary schools in the ways they were arranged and resourced. As in primary schools, students had a degree of choice between activities. In the ACS project, such choice was an important element of introducing genuine curriculum negotiation with pupils. The plan for a multi-skills base (see Fig. 2.3) illustrates the flexibility of such a teaching space. It shows an area which has sufficient space, appropriate furniture and flexibility for many different activities involving a class of about twenty students.

In one particular school the display area was used for a small group project 'Designing a mural'. This originated from an idea of decorating the base room, but it expanded to a more ambitious scheme. The group of young people and their tutors became involved in fundraising for money to finance the project; researching and costing materials, and finally producing the mural. The project spilled out of the school into industry when a local firm responded to the work done by subcontracting to the students the production of a mural in the work's canteen. The success of the multi base room does not rely on such ambitious projects, however. As may be seen from the plan, the central space can be used for whole group teaching as well as small group and individual project work to teach anything from basic English and maths to projects, individual assignments and discussion.

The arrangements of the base varied between schools. Work that was initiated in the base includes creative art, light craft, printing, pottery, silk screen printing and graphics, rural studies, life skills, computers, basic office skills, use of telephones, filing, typing and cataloguing. These activities are an invaluable way of demonstrating to reluctant learners the importance of basic communication and numeracy. One school ran a home skills course in their base, and students also learnt about basic electronics and repairs, home safety, painting and decorating, cooking and laundry.

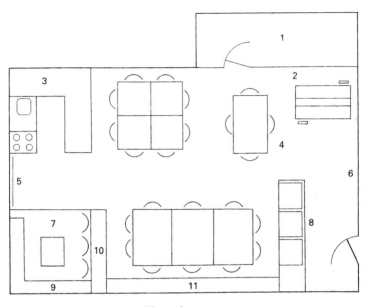

Key to the areas

1 Stockroom with lockable cupboards   7 Carpeted area
2 Display wall   8 Study booths
3 Kitchen units   9 Bench seating
4 Art and light craft   10 Shelves
5 White screen   11 Bookshelves etc.
6 Display area

Figure 2.3 Design for a multi-skills base (approximately 90m²)

The design and resourcing of the bases succeeded in creating a sense of security and belonging for the students, and many spoke of 'feeling like part of a big family'. This atmosphere was important for the success of particular courses being taught such as one on health education, when issues of parenthood and personal health care were explored. The role of the teacher in this new learning environment changes radically. There is a move away from teacher-centred and teacher-directed work towards the teacher becoming a facilitator and enabling perhaps as many different learning processes to take place as there are students in the group.

The teacher must be prepared for, and able to cope with, spontaneous development; must allow and encourage young people to work according to their own interests; and provide opportunities for those with initiative to plan and direct their own learning programme. By increasing the range of available experiences and resources for students to learn from the local community outside, the teacher becomes a pivot, around whom learning develops.

Critical observers of the 'multi-skills bases' in operation may misinterpret the activities which they see as being haphazard and unconnected. Experience has shown that teachers operating in this environment need to be better organized, more involved and more aware of pupils' individual needs than 'traditional' teachers. Record-keeping by teachers becomes crucial, in both plotting the skills and knowledge which a young person has acquired and the context in which they were demonstrated, and the directions in which he or she needs to move next.

As one of the project workers said:

Young people may need time to adjust to such an environment. This will be true while such spaces are unusual in our secondary schools, but we hope that they will soon become the norm. For the moment, however, young people need to be led into the new ways of working which the new environment will allow. Often young people, in traditional classes, are not allowed to develop the sort of autonomy which they deserve as young adults, and which they need if they are to cope with an increasingly complex society.

The multi-skills base increases motivation and attainment on the part of young people disenchanted with school. Young people begin learning about relating to adults in a more positive way in such an environment, seeing them as guides and mentors and not simply as authority figures.

In conclusion, the evidence of the ACS project demonstrates that multi-skills bases provide for students three major elements in successful learning: a secure environment for them to work and learn in different ways, the support and guidance of a tutor, while allowing for some independence, scope for flexibility and spontaneity, and opportunities to develop socially and academically, adaptation to individual needs and interests.

Structured play: the railway station

HELEN STRAHAN

As responsibility is handed back to the learner, the teacher–pupil relationship changes. It does not matter whether the students are infants, at the late secondary stage, or beyond statutory provision trying to become independent learners. The method has positive consequences. The experience of structured play seemed to lead the children to become more demanding learners in the class situation and to the teachers questioning their own practice. The Junior child who asked her teacher, 'What do you think I would be learning if you were in it?' was met by the response, 'I am in it . . . alongside you, really, learning things that you are learning.'

The structured play report is included here to point to the many parallels and shared commitments between teachers operating at opposite ends of the age range. Similar principles to those in evidence in the earlier reports seem to have led to the establishment of this 'station area' within the school.

In September 1986 I was given a year's secondment to undertake Manchester Polytechnic's Certificate in Educational Action Enquiry course, with the specific brief of looking at structured play as a cross-curricular approach to learning throughout the primary school. Structured play was not defined in any way and this, therefore, left scope for fairly open-ended enquiry.

For various reasons I decided to work in my own school on a whole school project. I started this by discussing play and its uses in school, with colleagues in both Infant and Junior departments. Two major concerns emerged from these discussions. First, a general regret that play, which is widely regarded as being of major importance for child development and learning, is progressively devalued as children move through the primary school. Second, a wish to foster children's control of their own learning, coupled with a recognition that in play children generally control their own activity, and that play could thus be a potentially valuable resource.

We decided that in the interests of continuity it would be most useful to start the project in the Infant department, with a view to later extension into the Junior department, and that an effective way of beginning to address the above concerns was to utilize a central space which was nobody's class base and was visible to most of the open plan Infant department, as a structured play area. At this point we took 'structure' to mean something in line with Manning and Sharp's interpretation. In the Schools' Council project *Structuring Play in the Early Years at School* (Manning and Sharp, 1977) they sought to link the theory of play to practice and defined structuring as the provision of space, time and materials, and the acceptance of an active role by the teacher. They also stressed the importance of observing children's spontaneous play and the necessity of giving them freedom of choice. We decided that we wanted to go a little further than this and also allow children access to decision-making processes about their play environment.

The staff made one fundamental decision without consulting the children – that a railway station would be a suitable theme for the play area because it tied in with the general departmental theme of 'movement'. However, having done this and cleared the proposed area in readiness, it seemed an appropriate time to hand responsibility to the children. The first step in this process was to take them all to Piccadilly station (in very small groups) and to take plenty of photographs of the experience, thus ensuring that everyone had knowledge, informed opinions and access to records.

We followed this by two large conferences to share our experiences and ideas for our proposed 'station' play area. Teachers chaired these discussions and acted as scribes for brainstorming. These conferences led to a period of intensive child/child, teacher/child and teacher/teacher negotiation as to what each class should be responsible for in the school station.

The station area began with a very basic train made of upturned staging, two telephones, a ticket office, plastic money, various bags, wallets and purses, a guard's uniform, blank British Rail timetables, posters and writing materials. The children were timetabled to use the play area in class groups of up to fifteen and were constantly changing the environment – items were repositioned and resources made or acquired as needs were identified.

By the end of several weeks the basic train had seats, a driver's compartment, hardboard sides with windows and a guard's van. The station had a platform, telephone kiosks, a clock, a sweet shop, all sorts of signs and information notices, a lost property office and an archway and ticket collector's booth at the entrance. All sorts of relevant items were available, for example, a whistle, flags, a tape of train noises, newspapers and magazines in several languages and a porter's trolley.

It had been agreed by all staff that, although this was essentially a collaborative and experimental venture, certain learning experiences could be predicted. Mathematical activity would take place when buying and selling tickets, planning timetables, telling the time and calculating distances and times of arrival. The availability of a wide range of reading and writing materials would lead to the station being an environment conducive to literacy activity. Social skills would be important, children would have to share, organize and co-operate. We also agreed that we should make every effort to monitor both our own and the children's behaviour. This monitoring was carried out by using simple observation sheets, audio and video taping and by interviewing participants and outside observers.

The following are some of the major conclusions that we drew from these monitoring activities:

1 All the predicted learning experiences had occurred and many had been developed in different directions by the children

2 Children sustained play for longer than expected with little teacher intervention

3 There was little argument between children, the use of co-operation and negotiation to resolve conflict was seen in all age groups

4 Children of all abilities played together in a supportive way – nobody appeared to feel that they were 'better' or 'worse' at playing than anyone else

5 The play area was a useful place in which to get children from different age groups interacting

6 The older children were often seen to play in groups of three or four and there was evidence of high quality sustained discourse between children

7 The teacher's most useful role often appeared to be that of observer who used knowledge thus gained to provide materials or ideas. When the teacher assumed too high a profile children did not explore their own ideas or engage in sustained interaction or conversation

8 There was a lot of evidence of people having fun. Children and staff seemed to enjoy the sometimes hard work involved in planning, creating and playing in the station. They had to co-operate with peers and others and take responsibility for their actions, yet nobody refused either explicitly or implicitly to become involved; motivation seemed high

Three major questions also arose which we felt had to be addressed:

1 Should teachers have specific goals for sessions or is *post hoc* rationalization acceptable?

2 Could we extend these sorts of play activities into individual classes?

3 How were we going to involve Junior staff and children in structured play?

As regards (1), this is something that continues to cause concern, but the consensus of opinion that seems to be emerging is that if we favour a model of curriculum as process rather than product, and really believe in the importance of making school a meaningful environment in which children engage in relevant activities, then we must, at least occasionally, be prepared to learn with and from the pupils, and not always start with all the answers. We should therefore be prepared for children to spend some time each week playing in an area in which learning outcomes are left sometimes to chance and sometimes to the interest of the children and/or teacher.

The second question is also still being addressed. It seems that the experience of the station area has led to children becoming more demanding learners in the class situation and teachers becoming more questioning of their own practice. The railway station experiment lasted from October to January, during which time it served as a useful focus. Since then the staff have been setting up various situations in their own classes and developing and refining ideas.

Junior involvement in the project has evolved in various ways. Just before dismantling the railway station, we organized several joint Top Infant and younger Junior sessions there. These fostered continuity of approach by creating a focus for staff to discuss their perceptions and attitudes to the primary curriculum in general and play in particular, and to find many common concerns. By introducing children from different departments to each other in an informal and non-threatening way gave Junior children and staff firsthand knowledge of an Infant department learning experience. They also reversed the tendency when looking at Infant and Junior continuity to ensure that the Infants visit the Juniors but not vice versa. Here we saw Junior children returning to the Infant department as learners, not as superior beings who have outgrown the academic resources on offer.

While this Junior involvement was occurring, an older Junior class were also being drawn in. Some of them had acted both as outside and as participant observers of the Infant play and had become very interested both in what the Infants were doing and in setting up their own structured play area in the Junior building. They subsequently became architects and organizers of an extremely democratic process whereby every child in the Junior department had a say as to whether they should have a structured play area, what form this should take and how it should be set up. This Junior action stemmed from an explicit realization that the Infant children had a large measure of freedom in setting up their structured play area and that they enjoyed using it because in a very real sense they owned that environment.

I do not think it would be unreasonable to claim that the project has been a learning experience for all those involved – the following is taken from an interview between a Junior child and her class teacher:

Child: What do you think you would be learning if you were doing structured play?

Teacher: I am doing structured play.

Child: No – if you were in it.

Teacher: I am in it and I am learning things, because I've not really done structured play before so I'm learning things from it as well. Er – I'm learning how to – alongside you really, things that you're learning like sociability and how to set things up and how you can bring it into, into school and make people realize that it's not play as in when we go outside and have a run round – that it's worthwhile and it leads onto other things here in school and that all areas of our school day can be brought into structured play.

The 'Mansfield Park' project

MARGARET HOWARD

In this report we move from the infant classroom to A-level work. It appears, however, that very similar worries that some have about 'play' as an effective medium for real learning, are reflected here in conventional measures of successful learning. In this report there is no immediate and drastic change to the physical learning environment. What we do find is a teacher prepared to shift her approaches to the use of time, space, outside agencies and 'who is in charge'. With these changes, the perceived nature of the environment for learning and the nature of learning seems to change.

The incorporation of the student as a peer learner, at least to some extent, leads to the acceptance of comment on the teaching process. The teacher begins to change by reflecting on this helpful information. 'You are not teaching like you . . . ' leads to a discussion about the whole process of teaching, more especially of teaching a novel that none of them particularly liked. Learning through reformulating the novel by means of drama, and supported structurally through an accreditation system leads to a shift in the teacher's role. 'My role was very much that of a resource; when they needed specific help they got it, but as I had suspected would happen, they were perfectly competent to help themselves.'

When space, time and resources are used in new ways in school, anxieties erupt, which increase the possibilities for change. A-level students began to worry about not having notes, just as ACS students questioned whether they were doing real work if they were not filling their writing books. Were other groups learning more? The teacher had to face the insecurities of the staff room; 'that's all very nice but they still have to pass their A-levels.' The teacher who is experimenting has to take this questioning of professional judgement. She may also have to ride out the storms of disruption when everybody is disturbed by an unintended consequence of the innovation. Disruption of school routines, for example where modular courses are introduced, will also cause an initial backlash from uninvolved members of staff. Not all possibilities can be prepared and planned for.

It is at the point where links with the formal curriculum are strongest that change can be most readily valued, or paradoxically prove most difficult. The only success indicator may be – do the students do better? It will not be enough to say 'they did no worse, but enjoyed it more and learned many things not examined at GCSE or A-level'. The initiative is expected to validate itself in conventional terms, better grades for instance. If support is recruited initially within the department and a team approach is engaged, survival of the innovation is more likely. If structural links such as the unit credit system which spreads across the curriculum are involved so much the better. The A-level English experiment raised the profile and status of the scheme as well as providing a motivating 'fall-back' position for students. Because it was modular, the unit could then be on offer to other students, including a wide range of people perhaps outside the department's remit. The student portfolio was enlarged, another possibility for choice offered.

The 'Mansfield Park' project is an attempt to approach A-level English literature texts in a way that involves the students in more active learning, is much wider in its scope of learning experiences than traditional methods, and represents a modular development to the A-level syllabus. It is also an attempt to make the course more exciting and relevant to the individual experiences of the students, and to introduce a more practical dimension and a multi-skills approach into a course that can very easily become sterile, and justifiable only in an exceedingly narrow context.

For a long time, I had been very concerned that A-level students can work for two years, produce class and homework that demonstrates a range of skills and abilities, yet, at the end of that two-year period, fail to gain a pass grade in the final examination – and more to the point, gain no credit at all for their achievements within those two years. A breakdown of the A-level syllabus into a series of modules that allow for a much wider range of experience than is traditional for the A-level English literature course, and that would receive Northern Examining Association unit accreditation, would be a way of ensuring that, whatever the final outcome, students would be given credit for what they had achieved. Drawing up the modules is also an excellent exercise for the teachers involved, as they necessitate a clear focusing on the specific skills and learning areas that we are working towards developing.

It was against this background that my students and I wanted to explore an alternative method of approaching the text that was set for that year – Jane Austen's *Mansfield Park*. We had 'done' two pages of the novel when one of the students said 'You're not teaching like you used to', so I put the novel down, and we talked as a group about the whole process of teaching, and more particularly, of teaching a novel that, although they had all read, none of them really liked. What came out of the discussion was that the best way to overcome the question of liking or not liking – which is, in a sense, irrelevant – was to transfer the teaching to the students themselves. Originally, we had no ideas about developing a module; we were just looking for an alternative approach, but so much work went into the process, and so many skills came to light, that we wrote the module in retrospect.

We decided that the students would share control of their learning, and would work on producing a workshop, with a teaching pack, to be taken out of the classroom and shown to other students working on the same text. We had recently seen Box Theatre Company's *Macbeth*, and wanted to work in the same way – a five minute version (which is an excellent way to summarize plot, and identify key incidents), and a series of dramatized themes. We were very lucky, because when we approached the English inspector, he allowed us to have members of the Box Theatre Company come into school on a regular basis, and work with the students on dramatic techniques. That has been particularly useful in the sense that I learned an enormous amount from them.

I must say, at this stage, that the whole project took only the same amount of class time that would be devoted to any A-level text, and did not need, other than the initial 'training' by Box, any special funding, teaching areas, or resources, other than those the students themselves supplied. The other important point is that although this approach did culminate in a performance, none of the students were forced to take part in the performance; there were lots of other areas where they could contribute. From a group of thirteen students, eight chose to perform, and five preferred to work on writing the handout, arranging for printing, arranging the venue, helping with scripts, working on costumes and symbols, and so on. The Box Theatre members usually came in class time, and worked with different groupings from the thirteen.

The actual process involved the students getting together as a whole group and deciding, first, what they thought were the most important aspects of the novel. We did a lot of group discussion, but from beginning to end the students were in control. My role was very much that of a resource; when they needed specific help, they asked for it, but as I suspected, they were on the whole perfectly competent to help themselves. They had access to the library, and to other staff for background information, and they had the novel itself – but this time it was theirs, not mine, and that switch of emphasis was vitally important. I also worked as a liaison between the different groupings, and between the students and the theatre group. We tried to build in a weekly evaluation session, but we were not strict enough about this in our first attempt, and suffered the consequence later.

As this group was one of five within the college, there were obvious pressures on the students involved. Initially, they were all very enthusiastic, but as more people heard about what they were doing, and began to comment on the project, they began to feel insecure, and worried about passing the A-level examination. They were concerned about not having notes from the teacher – that came up time after time – and thought that other groups might be learning more. The second time we used this approach, I was much more aware of what they might face from outside the group, and prepared the students for it, but the first time, with *Mansfield Park*, we did have problems. I told them then, and still maintain, that the learning process in our education system is far too teacher-dependent, and it is vital, given the context of the world outside the classroom, that they take responsibility for their own learning, and in fact, stop thinking in terms of the classroom as the place where they learn everything. The students, despite their fears, voted to continue with the project, but the pressure did unsettle them, particularly those who had voted not to take part in performance, and put them under more pressure than was necessary.

Another mistake I made was to let the division between the 'writers' and the 'actors' become too pronounced, so that actors became an élite, and the writers tended to feel left out. There were not enough whole group sessions, which would have prevented this, and again, the second time round, I was ready for this, and kept the whole group working together more.

As their teacher, I too was under a lot of pressure – as anyone who has attempted alternative teaching strategies will immediately recognize. I had to cope with a lot of 'That's all very nice, but they still have to pass their A-levels . . . ' and 'I still think when it comes down to it they need notes from the teacher.' That is entirely predictable, but it is something one has to be prepared to accept. Interestingly, when the students sat their mock examinations, they all scored far more highly on the *Mansfield Park* questions than on anything else on the paper! Also, part of the workshop involved the whole group coming forward at the end of the performance to answer questions from the audience, and that was very gruelling for a group of students. They had to deal with set questions for which they had not been prepared other than by themselves, and they dealt with them magnificently.

When the students were ready to take the workshop out, they wrote to the colleges and schools whose students they thought might like to see it, and arranged for an evening venue. Again, we were lucky, in that a Manchester high school's Alternative Curriculum Strategies' students had converted a prefab in their school grounds into a small theatre, and they were happy for us to use their theatre for our venue. We have our own drama studio, but I think it is very important for students to take the workshop out of their own environment, and be prepared to move around. To add a sense of occasion, we served wine after the workshop, and we had a small group of students from the Royal Northern College of Music to play at the beginning and the end. These two features were an added luxury, but neither is outside the reach of most schools; tea or coffee would have been fine, which could involve some cross-curricular work with the home economics department, and most schools could supply the music more cross-curricular work. The possibilities for cross-curricular work are endless.

The final workshop really was impressive, and as this was a new approach to A-level, interested members of the Inspectorate also came, so the students were coping with a very high level of questioning from the audience. The whole thing was on video, giving both a permanent record, and a resource for any interested schools who want to use the video. After the workshop had been performed, we itemized the learning areas and outcomes, and wrote them up as a unit credit, which has since been validated and is available for use through the NEA as an approach to the study of any novel.

I have since used this same approach to study *Lord of the Flies*, and would like, briefly, to describe the changes that I think has made this second attempt more successful. First, we were, the second time, working from the unit, which has differentiated outcomes. All students must complete the first 'block', and then choose from a selection of outcomes. Because the choices are much more structured now the unit is available, this has prevented the growth of an 'élite' group. Also, with *Lord of the Flies*, I have changed the groups round far more often, so that every student (and this is with a group of sixteen), has worked on every theme. This time the students have chosen to use far more technical resources, such as background slides, their own video work, more taped music, and so on – but they have been entirely responsible for the use of these.

We have also taped evaluation sessions, and have been very strict about regular group evaluation, after each working session. Again, this has prevented the break-up of the group into cliques, and has ensured that everybody has had a chance to express their feelings – sometimes very forcibly, but that has been an extremely valuable part of the learning experience. As it happens, the whole group wanted to take part in the performance – not easy with a large group, but they have achieved it – so the whole group has tackled most of the outcomes. Finally, the students worked on their own far more this time, as we did not have the input of a theatre group, although obviously I had the benefit of that experience, so the workshop, although perhaps less polished, is very much their own thing.

What have the students gained – and what has the teacher gained – from this method? I can perhaps best answer that by saying that one of last year's students has come into college on a voluntary basis, and has worked with this year's group with absolute confidence. Self-esteem and confidence have to be the two key words, together with responsibility for self, and for the group (and in the competitive field of A-level work this quality is rare), and there has developed, among us all, a much greater sense of sharing a task. The very artificial divisions between teacher and learners have been broken down, since the roles have been reversed, so the whole learning environment has changed. We saw an old film of *Lord of the Flies* a week after our own workshop had been recorded on video – 'They've stolen our ideas!' cried my students, indignantly . . .

Pilot scheme in GCSE mathematics
ADRIAN HARRINGTON

The final report in this section might seem to involve very little, if anything at all, in the way of changes to the learning environment. To some readers, however, it is here that their sense of schooling as usual might be most disrupted; in the structured, ordered, world of mathematics teaching. What the report emphasizes is how this group of teachers, with their commitment to investigative approaches in mathematics, attempted to create an environment in which the students could begin to evolve and develop their own ideas. The report also conveys the extent to which such a scheme required the active and continuing involvement of the staff.

My school is an 11–18 comprehensive with a predominantly working-class catchment area. It has approximately 1,300 pupils, but this is soon to be reduced with the loss of our sixth form due to an Authority reorganization. The school as a whole is active in many ways, with strong community links and a reputation for involvement in innovations on various fronts.

The mathematics department has a set of rooms arranged together in a single building, together with a small staffroom and three storerooms. Historically, the department has been involved in research work, looking at teaching methods and investigative approaches in mathematics. It has developed strong links with the Association of Teachers of Mathematics and the Shell Centre for Mathematical Research.

The department saw a departure of perhaps the most active innovators, two to become advisory mathematics teachers and the other to take up a research post at the Shell Centre. The management of the school supported the appointment of a new head of department and a deputy head of department who had similar philosophies and who wished to continue in the same vein. Early on in their appointment an opportunity to join a pilot General Certificate in Secondary Education was made available. It was in a wave of enthusiasm and 'naivety' that the department was launched towards this radically new scheme.

The GCSE syllabus we opted for offers the full range of grades and differentiation is by outcome, using tasks which match the ability of the candidates. The students produce a folio of work which may contain extended pieces of work; notes related to oral work, evidence of practical work, evidence of candidates' ability to evaluate their own work, evidence of group work, diaries and so on.

Assessment of the folio is done with reference to seven objectives, as follows:

1 Communication – ability to present mathematics, orally, visually, practically or in continuous prose
2 Implementation – ability to prepare and carry out the task using suitable techniques and skills
3 Mathematical knowledge – ability to create, refer to and use a wide range of facts, concepts and skills
4 Interpretation – ability to see the implications of the work done
5 Evaluation – ability to reflect on her or his own work
6 Autonomy – ability to take responsibility for her/himself and the direction of her or his own learning
7 Mathematical attitude – the candidates' appreciation of the possibilities and power of mathematics.

An important strength of this syllabus is this method of assessment. Because the grading is fundamentally summative, the grade awarded for each criterion is given for the whole two years' work. Single pieces of work do not have the effect of dragging a grade down, because the grade awarded is seen as the point at which the pupil can consistently work by the end of the fifth year. The median grade of the seven criteria is then taken. Again this has an important quality. An isolated low grade, for example, a 'G' in evaluation, does not mean that the overall grade is overly distorted. However, having said it is essentially a summative assessment, the framework can be used in a formative way. Because each piece of work is not averaged out, the pupil can truly demonstrate a development across the years four to five.

It was felt that none of the existing mode 1 syllabuses matched the department's needs. Even the most enlightened offered a maximum of 50 per cent coursework. External examinations as they stand in mathematics work strongly against the sort of methodology developed in our department. We felt that examinations encouraged a form of imitative mathematics – mathematics where the teacher presents a set method of solving a particular problem. These methods often make baffling leaps in logic and are, for the majority of pupils, very difficult to remember. It is also not an efficient way of learning. These methods often stand alone and even a pupil who can apply them is usually unable to solve a similar problem posed in a slightly different way. Rather than imposing someone else's way of tackling a situation, we felt it was far more effective for pupils to develop their own strategies and discover their own rules. Such a way into mathematics would allow pupils to evolve a firmer structure of understanding.

As a consequence of this philosophy we were no longer concerned with achieving the same response from the whole class, but a variety of responses on different levels. We could concern ourselves with assessing the process of solving problems and because of this, pupils' responses, no matter what the level, could be valued. Pupils could begin to enjoy problem solving for its own sake – the discovery, the struggle, the structuring.

It is probably useful at this stage to describe in more detail how the department attempts to achieve these ideas. At present we have mixed-ability groups in years one to four and hope soon to have mixed-ability through to the fifth year. The work in the fourth and fifth years is designed around activities and tasks which last for approximately three weeks (although this is not a rigid format). A problem or situation is set up which the pupils are asked to investigate. A typical example would be:

Given a 3×3 dot grid

Example   .   .   .

              .   .   .   gradient = 1/2

              .   .   .

a   How many different gradients are there on this grid?
b   What about a 4 × 4, 5 × 5, n × n grid?
c   What about rectangular grids?

These notes would not necessarily be given to the pupil but could form the support for a class teacher's introduction. From this basic starter the pupils have to work at developing their own ideas and questions. The criteria for such a starter is that the whole class can become initially involved in it and that it is rich enough to allow a variety of subsequent developments at a whole range of levels.

To teachers not experienced in working in this way the prospect of beginning a lesson with so little initial guidance is daunting. It is not just a matter of introducing the starter and leaving the class to it. The role of the teacher is still central. He or she has to work at understanding the pupil's ideas and responding to them in a supportive and non-directive way. Thus the teachers in the department have the task of creating an atmosphere in which the pupils can begin to evolve and develop their own ideas.

For the department this has been a very demanding time – both in developing our teaching approaches so that these values are communicated to the pupils and in terms of the extra workload created by the assessment – particularly since frequent feedback to the pupils is essential if they are to understand the criteria by which their work is assessed. Essential support has been provided by termly in-service weekends with the other pilot schools involved in this GCSE and representatives of the examining board. These are times when the interpretation of the assessment criteria are discussed and the moderation of awarding grades to these are dealt with. Much time is also spent sharing ideas and discussing issues. Even with a department as committed to this philosophy as ours is, there is a variety of teaching styles. We felt it was important for colleagues to interpret the philosophy and aims in terms of their own teaching approach. For some the change has been more drastic than others, and we are at present discussing ways of supporting each other through difficulties. Regular metings, where administration is kept to a minimum but where methodology is discussed, are essential. We meet formally at least once a week, and informally much more often.

Our second cohort of pupils has just begun in the fourth year, and some changes were made in the light of our experiences. One of the most important was that we decided not to set them as we had done previously, but to create mixed-ability groups. Although this decision was not easily made, it was felt that our lower-ability pupils often missed out by not being part of a group which 'buzzed' with ideas. They rarely saw the potential in some of the starting points and therefore needed the support of the teacher to keep activities going.

Although the evaluation of such a scheme is a continual process, some essential features have emerged. First, the need for regular feedback to pupils. Second, parents need to be kept informed and involved through open evenings, parents evenings, letters and so on. Third, constant support for staff is important to allow them to 'evolve' their own teaching styles, and the scheme must continually evolve through the active involvement of the staff. Finally, a realization that such a methodology cannot stand alone within a school. It is easy to become isolated within a large school and work must be done to share one's ideas and philosophy with the rest of the staff.

These issues are ones which we are still facing. There are no

easy answers to some of them because they involve the development of people. This evolution is slow and we must remind
ourselves that if change is to be lasting then it is the people
who must change, not the framework within which they work.
However, we now have a GCSE which to a large extent reflects
rather than dictates our methodology.

General comments

*In summary, changed settings within a school may begin as a physical re-
ordering of space, but can rapidly offer possibilities for social and structural
change. Even in the absence of major physical changes, teachers and students
can together exploit possibilities in the classroom. As the roles of each group
change, so the school itself can become a different sort of society.*

*There are two issues to which the reports in this chapter clearly point.
First, we have included here reports in the core areas of English and
mathematics. These, as well as the other reports, display how aspects of
cross-curricular dimensions, skills and themes can be addressed within
specific subject areas. Perhaps it will be matters associated with personal
and social education which will be most immediately obvious to readers,
but the development of cross-curricular skills – such as communication
skills, problem-solving skills and study skills – is also apparent. A central
concern, of course, is to look in a systematic way at how the range of
subjects, but also the range of learning environments within the school, can
be central resources for the effective implementation of the whole curriculum.*

*A second issue is the way in which some of the reports, particularly
those on business studies, design education and pottery, raise matters of
interest in relation to technology programmes of study within the National
Curriculum. Given that at each key stage pupils will be expected to design
and make environments (surroundings made or developed by people in
response to needs and requirements identified by them), there are some
powerful parallels with some of the teachers' concerns captured in the
reports.*

*Four of these case studies are practical examples of the way teachers
have designed environments in response to educational needs and requirements
that they have identified. This demonstrates an important shift of emphasis
from designing a curriculum that will fit into a classroom to designing a
'classroom' to fit the needs of the students and the curriculum.*

*It would be ironic if a National Curriculum intended to meet the needs
of the 1990s and beyond was constrained by having to fit into an environment
designed, in some cases, for the 1890s. Just as we are asking pupils to see
the connection between human purpose and design, so we should be asking*

what sorts of learning environments best suit the needs of the National Curriculum and the students to be educated within them.

3

Using Settings Outside the School

The residential

JEAN-PIERRE KIRKLAND

Residential courses have been a standard part of the education system for many years. This report is included because it emphasizes the potential variety of purpose which can be accomplished by a residential. The curriculum report describes in some detail the setting up and running of a residential course with a particular emphasis on personal and social education. The curriculum element is part of the standard school Personal and Social Education (PSE) course but 'school timetables . . . place severe constraints on longer-term developmental work' and the residential is seen as a way of providing an intensity and consistency of experience which is impossible within the normal school day.

Statements of aims in PSE courses can seem hopelessly vague and idealistic. This description, however, shows in some detail precisely how these aims might be realized. Once again there are claims that the 'out-of-school' experience is transforming for some pupils, 'school refusers or those whose attendance pattern has been very poor, have attended lessons far more frequently afterwards'.

It is also worth noting the concern to balance routine with flexibility within the course and the aside which hints at the strain which such courses place on normal school routines, 'of course up to thirty pupils absent from GCSE course work assignments is bound to create problems in all departments within the school'.

School timetables automatically place severe constraints on longer-term developmental work. In a school where personal and social education is based upon the concept of a continuing curriculum experience and where the lessons are essentially skills-based, developmental work becomes rather like chickens trying to break out of a reinforced shell, an interruption or a bell ringing prevent the hatching process from taking place so that unfinished business with all its implications is often the hallmark of the best planned courses. There will never be an ideal solution to the problem, but the idea of a residential course, some distance from the school and home and using the methodology of PSE can be a most effective way of exploring issues in considerable depth, while allowing for pupils, teachers and others to mix together informally in an atmosphere conducive to the growth of developmental processes.

At my high school the idea of residential experience grew out of a mixture of contemporary studies and PSE following reorganization in 1982. The first course took place in January 1983 and seven subsequent courses, now held at a scout camp in Mellor, near the Cheshire/Derbyshire boundary, have been organized since then for fourth-year pupils. Normally between twenty-five and thirty pupils are taken, from all abilities and an equal balance is left between male and female. Since the site is self-catering, a couple of former pupils act as cooks; a number of former pupils come along as facilitators for group discussion work, and parents plus other members of the community come for periods of time to suit themselves. The course normally lasts for five days with an advance group going down a day early to clean, set up equipment and welcome the main group the following morning. A shorter weekend course is also arranged, but the degree of depth to which issues can be taken is limited, or the number of issues to be looked at in-depth restricted. Both rate, however, amongst the most successful and significant experiences for pupils, ex-pupils, visitors and staff.

The first course was hurriedly thrown together in under three weeks; it used a lot of traditional PSE methods and followed a number of contemporary themes. It worked and it worked so well that it motivated staff to improve upon the first experience. A number of former pupils on that first course have since become facilitators on subsequent courses. The residential has now been fine-tuned and in the light of experience, constantly modified so that a highly successful learning environment is created to meet the ever changing needs of young people today. Useful help here was found in material by Leech and Wooster (1986).

The course at Mellor is built round a series of models or structures which are best represented in diagramatic form:

The six sections of Figure 3.1 require some amplification:

1   The atmosphere of the learning environment is created by a series of ice-breaking and warm-up activities, a series of confidence building and trust exercises, and by interpersonal group work which heightens the emotional awareness in

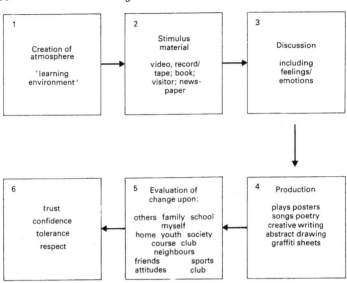

Figure 3.1   The residential

terms of the feelings and of the needs of everyone involved in the course.

2   The stimulus material is introduced in varying degrees over the three full days of the course, each day having a majority of the time devoted to a theme: Tuesdays are spent investigating addiction, and the stimulus material is a full-length film on video, a short documentary, newspaper and magazine articles and music; Wednesday's theme is aggression, and a full length film on video, a short documentary, poetry and songs are used as stimulus; Thursday is a decision-making day where the stimulus is largely people and songs, with a decision-making game being run by one of the larger banks who visit for that day. Choice of stimulus material is exceptionally important, and it must be constantly re-examined and if necessary changed.

3   Discussion after the stimulus is usually done in smaller groups, each group consisting of about nine or ten pupils, two or three facilitators, a visitor and a member of staff. The pupils' groups remain the same for the whole week, but the facilitators, staff and visitors change constantly. Occasionally large-group discussion, usually preceded by a brainstorming session, is more appropriate; for instance, after the film *Threads*, (which is about living through a nuclear holocaust),

when emotion is often running high, the large group can be a useful total sharing and caring experience.

4   The creative side of the course normally takes place in smaller groups, in pairs, or occasionally individually. Course members can be encouraged relatively easily to express their feelings, and show what they are learning, and explore further issues raised by the stimulus in a variety of ways – songs can be written and performed using well-known tunes; role play and drama can be rehearsed and produced, posters can be designed and displayed, along with poetry and creative writings, pupils may wish to express feelings on graffiti sheets or in the form of abstract drawings. All are appropriate media for everyone to observe and share in. There is such diversity of forms of expression that all can be used and should be employed in as open-ended a way as possible (many pupils often return to their 'piece of work' long after starting, usually in free time, in order to improve it, or complete it – is this is a common feature of the normal classroom?)

5   On a residential, constant evaluation and feedback is necessary, and this must be a shared experience so that the active learning process is constantly being reinforced. Further, it is an ideal place for the observation and examination of change as it is likely to affect everyone involved in the course. Goal-setting exercises can be used for measuring some changes while on the course. Other changes in attitude and outlook can be explored by discussion-based developmental groups which look at the self in terms of the wider life circle of school, community, society at large, the family and home, the neighbours, the friends, those on the course and any other areas where interpersonal relationships may be in need of reflection, (for instance, attitudes to equality of sexes, races, religion and so on.)

6   The evaluation of self, the course, the feedback of pupils, ex-pupils and staff, plus the general display of material which builds up over the days leads to an atmosphere of mutual understanding, of trust, of improved tolerance and of respect. It is a magic atmosphere within which to work, and as Figure 3.1 shows, we are now back at the beginning of the process, but this time at a much higher and at a much more intense level, and the journey around the circuit begins again. Each time the process is repeated, so the level is raised and the degree of active learning increased.

A typical day at the residential, as portrayed in Figure 3.1, may well start at 7.00 a.m. with voluntary aerobics or jogging

(1). After breakfast, there will be simple warm up games (1). Stimulus material may be a film such as *French Connection II*, with a coffee break. (2). This could be followed by a large group discussion centred on a brainstorm sheet, followed by smaller groups looking at three separate areas of addiction taken from illegal drugs, smoking, prescribed drugs, alcohol and gambling (3). The groups decide what to produce (4), songs, drama, poetry or posters, perhaps. Further stimulus material is made available. After lunch, the groups work on their task and then produce the result for all the participants. After a tea break, some music is added, or a documentary, and the groups then think about the effects of what they have seen or done on themselves, the family, community and society at large. They discuss how they feel about particular issues and what changes they could make if any are necessary (5). After dinner, the return is to atmosphere-building again with sessions designed to help foster trust, build confidence and develop other spiritual qualities using the idea of writing a play and performing it, watching a short video and designing posters, individually or collectively, and doing some creative writing. Each night, each group of ten embarks upon a different activity together. After dinner, lighter relief is provided by a comedy video, a musical session or extended games. A final evaluation session for pupils is followed by a nightwalk after which the staff have their own debriefing with facilitators.

Running such an involved course does present problems. Some of these are simple organizational ones – getting all the materials together and in the right order, remembering the equipment, collecting money, doing the shopping and so forth. Experience tends to overcome these. Other more complicated problems occur in terms of finance, and so far pupils have had to pay only about half the total cost, so that any form of discrimination on a financial basis has been kept to a minimum. However, deciding which pupils are to go (demand always exceeds supply) is an annual headache, and involves a complicated mixture of first come, first served, coupled with who deserves to go balanced by keeping numbers equal in the sexes. Drawing names from a hat as a last resort, is not ideal. But no one is discriminated against on grounds of either ability or behaviour, although some parents do use the latter from time to time. As the conditions of employment of teachers change, so difficulties arise in releasing staff for a full week, and of course up to thirty pupils absent from GCSE coursework assignments is bound to create problems in all departments within the school. As much advance warning as possible is given of the courses so that staff can plan deadline dates within their departments around the week away. But the spin-offs for the whole school of pupil involvement in the life of the school generally, in terms of attendance and in terms of much improved attitudes, far outweigh any of the disadvantages. A similar effect is noticed among the staff too. As for ex-pupils, there is almost always a waiting list of those wishing to join the courses as facilitators. And that says a lot for the enduring quality of the week.

Link courses

LORNA BORLAND

This curriculum report was chosen because it is based on a co-operative venture between two or more educational institutions. A distinction is sometimes made between the educational world and the 'real world'. There are important ways in which educational institutions can offer 'real world' experiences to pupils.

The description of the link course developments at a local community college illustrates a number of important concerns. The first is with the ad hoc *nature of much 'out-of-school' provision. The report traces the development from the early 'link' course, which used up spare capacity in the college to offer courses to school pupils, to an organized programme with a college co-ordinator and an administrative structure. The* ad hoc *arrangements led to either 'very good or very bad' courses with children 'voting with their feet' and not attending or attending only spasmodically. These are problems which are echoed elsewhere. The theory of 'out-of-school environments for learning' is all very well and many schools would be able to point to good practice but the questions are how is the best practice maintained and the general quality of such experiences improved. One answer is illustrated in this report. The 'out-of-school' element must generate its own routines, there must be common expectations among all involved and, perhaps most importantly, there must be a common investment of time and interest. The worst courses may be those being run by 'part-time lecturers' who are interested in filling their teaching hours but 'do not really wish to teach school pupils.'*

The benefits claimed range from improved attitude and commitment 'when they are able to spend some time away from that [the school] environment each week to improved teacher–pupil relationships and improved transition from school to college'.

This report is important because it makes apparent the considerable administrative load involved in making 'out-of-school experience' part of the standard curriculum.

Throughout the period of one of the new initiatives in education, namely the Alternative Curriculum Strategies project (ACS) which took place in Manchester between 1982–86, link courses had been operating on an *ad hoc* basis. Many colleges had offered slack time on their timetables in certain departments, to schools. This helped the colleges with student numbers while giving some schools the chance of using better facilities or equipment in a post-16 college. There had also been a few link courses which had developed over the years, mainly with sixth forms in schools.

Experience in the ACS project, which had built in to its submission funding for schools' links with colleges, showed that the courses offered had no specific level of skill or learning, and that little thought had been given to the aims and objectives of the particular course apart from the actual experience of attending a college. These courses were sometimes offered by a college and then when taken up, schools found that the course had been handed over to a part-time lecturer who did not really wish to teach school pupils aged between fourteen and sixteen, but who was glad of the extra teaching hours during the week. The courses tended to be either very poor or extremely good, depending upon the commitment, personality and interest of the particular lecturer. The courses were often offered with no prior planning – the college being mainly interested in extracting some extra funding from the new sources provided by schools. On poor courses, pupils voted with their feet and did not attend after the first week, or only attended spasmodically when pressure was applied from school.

One course which was run on several occasions illustrates the problems. This was an engineering course of thirteen weeks duration. The pupils were timetabled to attend for two hours in the morning and two hours in the afternoon on a particular day of the week. The pupils were being asked to make a specific item such as a teapot stand, using wrought iron and a tile. The lecturer did not wish to teach school pupils or young people who were not specially interested in engineering as a career. The pupils were not interested in what they were being asked to make. The lecturer wanted students who were interested in the specific skills used in engineering, but the pupils wanted to make something which they felt would be of use to them. Part-time lecturers were used on many occasions and found the work a 'bind'. The level of work was too technical for the pupils and the lecturer, who was an engineer, had no patience with the pupils who did not understand what he was talking about or asking them to do.

This is not to say, however, that one or two departments within the colleges did not do a thorough job of their particular link courses. It became obvious through these few good courses that much benefit could be gained by pupils attending colleges for a short period each week, and having student status during this time. These pupils gained in self-confidence and were sometimes only attending the college course, and not attending school. Clearly some rationalization was needed. It was, first of all, important to set down some principles for these link courses.

Link courses should aim to give pupils the opportunity of learning in a new environment for a short period each week. By choosing courses, they would learn to negotiate a short modular course of study using equipment and techniques not readily available in school. In addition, link courses should allow pupils to take responsibility for themselves in a place other than school, for example, finding her or his way there, being punctual and so on. Attending a college would enable pupils to get a feel for the status of students before leaving school, and perhaps motivate them to follow a college course in the future. It would provide them with the opportunity to try courses in a college as tasters, before making a choice when moving on to a college after school. By experiencing several of these short courses during the last two years of schooling, they might discover not only what they do *not* wish to follow up in the future, but also where their real interest might lie.

A set of procedures was developed which came directly from the experiences and needs of both the schools and the colleges. This involved joint planning to relate school and college courses, careful briefing of tutors and students, the construction of clearly defined modules with unit accreditation, and monitoring by school and college staff of student experiences and progress.

Experience has shown that college links must have certain elements if they are to be successful. They must be aimed at the correct level and have plenty of practical work. They should use equipment or materials not readily available in school and use an approach which is different from school. It is important to give pupils student status while in the college and to assist them to make relationships within the college, for example, allowing them to have a coffee break in the college coffee bar along with the students. There is a need for school staff to come to the college and display interest and involvement in the college course. From this can come the possibility of follow-up work in the school, as well as the possibility in some courses of a link with what is already happening in school.

An example of a good link course developed during the past two years is that of a fast-food module. Meetings had taken place as detailed in the criteria, and a Northern Examination Association unit was designed to meet the requirements of the pupils and the department. The school was sent a copy of the course description sheet prior to the booking so that pupils opting for this particular course knew exactly what they were going to do. Built into the unit credit from the second week, was some negotiation between the lecturer and the pupils so that the pupils felt that they had some choice within the course. The lecturer had developed the course and so was not being presented with work which she had had no hand in developing, or had no interest in. The unit has been used as a discrete unit of work and also has been used by another school as part of a mainstream home economics GCSE course where pupils visited the college for one block (six weeks) in the two year GCSE course. This particular unit is presently used three times each week with different school groups and is always well attended, and both lecturer and school teachers (who take an active part as students) enjoy the experience.

We have also learned that some pupils need to be familiarized with the college, and threatening experiences need to be avoided in the following sorts of ways. First, the co-ordinator of the college link courses and/or lecturer in a specific department may visit the school to meet groups of pupils in tutor groups, personal and social education lessons or in careers lessons, but not in full-year assemblies. Past experience has proved this to be the least beneficial to both schools and colleges. Second, the groups of pupils should be welcomed on their first attendance to a course by the college co-ordinator and also a person from the student services section. The pupils should be shown round the college and given general information. Much of the threatening experience is avoided by this being done while the pupils are with their own friends in the group, not facing a strange college alone. Finally, lunch may be arranged at the college (using school dinner tickets), and pupils may use the student coffee bar during breaks.

From my own experience and from talking to teachers in seven of the local schools using the link courses, I was able to ascertain the main benefits for the school and pupils. The pupils seem to work more readily, on the whole, in school when they are able to spend some time away from that environment each week. There is a better pupil–teacher relationship when pupils and teachers work alongside each other on college courses, learning subjects which are new to both of them. The pupils seem to gain in maturity after a short time spent attending college courses, and this has been noticed by the staff in schools. The short courses lend themselves to being accredited by the NEA so that pupils gained unit credits on college courses which they could then add to a Letter of Credit gained in school. Pupils enjoy courses and then gain some certification for it as well. Many pupils felt less threatened when leaving school and attending college when they had some familiarity with the surroundings beforehand. Pupils also have much more idea of what is required of them on college courses post-16 and what courses are most suitable for them. Through providing additional places for special needs pupils, some profoundly deaf or handicapped pupils have benefited from working alongside pupils from mainstream schools. The school pupils have also gained by this experience, which is one that we are developing through links with support teachers in special education.

Once the link courses were running well, it became obvious that there were many advantages for the college and lecturers other than those which had been seen in the past. When pupils enjoy a good link course they are more likely to come back to the college, and indeed to bring along friends or associates post-16. The pupils have already started the process of decision-making before leaving school, so there is more likelihood of them choosing the particular college if they feel at home there already. The short modular courses can be tasters for the post-16 courses, thereby giving pupils a real taste of what is to come. The student drop-out rate is reduced. The college is helped by the enhanced relationship with the staff in the schools who, in their turn, gained actual knowledge of the content of the post-16 course first hand.

Once the courses had started running in our local colleges, seven schools were using thirty-four link courses each week during 1986–87, with over 350 pupils attending college each week. It became very important to develop an administrative structure which would assist both schools and the college. There needed to be good communication between the schools and the college regarding students and pupils, and also the course content. To this end I developed a Link Course Pack which is available from Manchester Education Committee (see Fig. 3.2). From this pack you will see that we have endeavoured to look at the problems and needs of both schools and colleges. Termly meetings between the link course staff and the curriculum deputies of the schools is, therefore, seen as an important part of the scheme. These meetings lead to a better understanding of each other's problems.

Figure 3.2 College post-16 Link Course package
Devised by Lorna Borland, designed by Hilary Edwards

This package has been devised for use by colleges when running schools' Link Courses.

The sheets and cards are to be used as follows:

Sheet 1

Course Description Sheet

This will be completed by the department offering the Link Course, so that schools can see what a course entails. Schools may also wish to include details from this sheet in their school brochures for the information of parents.

When a course is already a validated Unit Credit, then a copy of the Unit Credit may be attached to the sheet instead of completing the course content part.

Sheet 2

School Attendance Sheet

This will be completed once a course has been accepted by a school and a date fixed for it to run.

The sheet will be sent to schools for each year group involved. It should be returned to the college department before the beginning of a course. This will ensure that pupils do not change courses without permission or exchange courses with pupils whilst a course is running.

Course tutors will complete the attendance sheet the first week also completing college Enrolment Forms, showing this on the sheet. A check can be kept of Enrolment Forms completed by each pupil for each course to be forwarded on to the college administration for processing. College registers will also be completed each week.

This sheet may be photocopied by the schools for use as a weekly register if required.

Figure 3.2 continued

Sheet 3

Skills Checklist

This is for use either for a Unit Credit Course or simply a modular course. It is a clear way of indicating the tasks completed on a course and can be used as a method of sending the schools information for pupil profiling for '365' and B.Tech. courses, or part of a G.C.S.E. course, or Record of Achievement.

Sheet 4

Unit Credit Returns Sheet

This is for use by tutors to inform the college co-ordinator of the pupils who have completed enough work to gain a Unit Credit.

The Link Course Co-ordinator then needs to check with schools whether each pupil named has got a Unit Credit entry number at school. Any pupil not entered for Unit Credits by their own school will need to be entered by the college, and given a college entry number.

A photocopy of this form may be sent to the schools for this purpose.

Card A
School Card

This card will list all the courses the school will have running at the college each half-term, with number of pupils on each course, year group, site attended at college and hours involved each week.

The reverse side of the card will be used by the co-ordinator to keep a check on attendances each week of a course. This will enable the college to see whether courses are popular and when they are not, seek remedies or renegotiate the course with the school.

Card B
Course Card

This card will be used to show which schools used a particular course. Each school will have a box showing the number of weeks of a course, any cancellations, the rate per hour being charged (if any), materials charged and a total amount for invoicing.

The reverse side of the card will show any cancellations during the course and whether all Enrolment Forms have been completed.

Sheet 5

This sheet may be used by the Link Co-ordinator as a quick reference timetable showing each Link Course running for a particular half-term.

For the schools there are three major problems. First, time-tables have to be drawn up in April/May, so schools need to have some idea of when and how such time can be made available to them for link courses. Second, schools have been left high and dry when colleges have had to withdraw courses at the last minute (beginning of September), due to alterations in student numbers, staffing and so on at the college. Third, payment of courses from school capitation is very difficult, both for teaching time and materials for courses.

For the colleges, the main difficulties are that student numbers in September might alter radically and courses may have to be withdrawn at the last minute because of lack of staff. No money may be available to take on part-time lecturers to teach a particular subject, for example brickwork and printing. There is also a need for a structure within which to teach, to which the lecturer can relate.

Initially many link courses had been arranged for under-achieving youngsters on the ACS project, or City and Guilds 365, with just the odd course being arranged for sixth formers in a special area of study or interest. During the past eighteen months numerous courses have been set up for a wide ability range, from underachievers to mainstream groups using a link course as a module within a GCSE course. However, as the courses developed tend to be short half-term modules, there needs to be a level of commitment from the pupils as missing one session is too significant, and a NEA unit cannot be gained without full attendance.

It is becoming increasingly obvious that link courses may have to take two directions – the general course which pupils of all abilities can attend where they have the opportunity of attending a college and trying out new subjects and having new experiences, and the more subject specific course where pupils with particular abilities or aptitudes attend a specially devised link course which is a taster for the post-16 course in which the pupil is specially interested, for example computer aided drawing or catering.

There are moves at present to look at particular courses post-16 to see if it is possible to break these down into units which can be started and accredited in school and then followed up in college. In recent years much emphasis has been placed on progression, and these courses would certainly follow this emphasis. Much has yet to be done in this area, perhaps linking in to other forms of certification post-16. As our experience grows and positive advantages can be seen by both schools, colleges and the education service, link courses are beginning to be seen as a permanent part of the college work. Both staff and pupils are becoming more confident and have gained in many ways from the experience.

Nursery placements

FINN DELOUGHRY

This is a second curriculum report in which the outside environment is another educational institution. It has been chosen for the way it illustrates the value of and the difficulties in trying to affect stereotypical behaviour, whether that of 'the school pupil' or that of the 'hard man'.

The 'activities' programme at the school is described and commented upon with a particular focus on the programme of placements in 'nursery schools' for a period of community work experience. Although the organiz- ation of the scheme is described, considerable emphasis is placed not just on what the pupils were learning from the placements but on what staff learnt from watching those pupils operate in the new environment. Working in the nursery the pupils were 'required to become members of staff for the duration of the placement'. Taking on this adult role, however, was difficult and sometimes impossible in the presence of other pupils. 'Without the presence of their jeering and mocking "mates", pupils began to show adult caring behaviour'. By observing these changes, staff on the project began to draw conclusions about the forces which shape school behaviour generally. Schools, it is concluded, far from preparing pupils for adult life, may well contribute to fixing their behaviour in childishness.

Although the evidence is scattered, it is worth noting the instances which are given of the nursery placement leading to transformed behaviour as with the 'reputedly "hard man" who displayed unexpected, uncharacteristic tenderness'.

Purpose, design and organization

At our school we run an 'activities programme' which occupies one day per week for all pupils in the fourth and fifth years. An important general aim of this programme is to make available to the pupils experiences not otherwise possible to them through the medium of the basic curriculum. We put the emphasis on active and immediate, concrete experiences, wishing not to repeat or to extend the commonly passive and vicarious learning environments of their previous school years. To some degree we sought from each of the activities of our programme, a contribution toward each pupil's self-knowledge, to be gained in a variety of new and therefore 'demanding' contexts.

There are six half-terms in the year, so we ran our six activity programme through at half-termly intervals. Thus, in due course for his or her group, each pupil was required to spend one half-day per week for half a term in a nursery, at some stage of the year.

We divided the fourth year into two bands, each band containing six groups of fifteen pupils. The maximum of fifteen was dictated by the capacity of the minibus, for those activities on a morning of the week and the other band on an afternoon of another day. So the same nurseries were receiving pupils twice a week. That gave us, at any one time, fifteen pupils in eight nurseries. In total, each pupil could accumulate some twenty hours of nursery experience on full attendance.

Incidental, even accidental, features of this arrangement made possible certain kinds of comparative studies. They presented us with three slightly different circumstances which proved unexpectedly revealing.

In some instances, the pupil went alone to a school's nursery class. In other, larger primary schools with two nursery classes in separated rooms, two pupils were placed one with each of the classes but having little contact with each other while there. In just two cases, two pupils worked together in the same nursery class.

We were soon able to conclude that pupils were more likely to adapt to the demands of their tasks, if a 'mate' was not present. As examples, we can quote such statements as, 'He has been quite good up to now but today, with his friend away, he has really come out of his shell. It was like having an extra member of staff.'

Once aware of this occurrence we were subsequently able to counter it by ensuring that such 'doubles' were always a boy and girl together. Then, in these circumstances, we were alerted to the possibilities of respective sexual role-stereotyping. The staffs of the two schools in question were as alert as their colleagues elsewhere and saw to it that it did not happen.

In effect, the pupils were required to become members of staff for the duration of their placement. In simple terms, it provided every opportunity for a pupil to show how adult s/he could be, both in relationships with the staff of the nursery and in their responsibilities as 'teachers' of the children.

The nursery teacher had for each pupil the checklist 'tick sheet' of the kinds of activities nurseries undertake and of the kinds of experiences pupils were likely to encounter there. Examples of the latter are 'comforting', 'arbitrating' and 'toileting'. By this means, the pupil's achievement was recorded in up to twenty categories. Each pupil was visited by the placement tutor on every occasion of attendance, to discuss experiences with the pupil and to gain from the observations of the staff a full picture of the pupil's performance.

It might take some pupils all of their visits to complete all or most of the tasks of the checklist but many completed all categories in a couple of visits and then set about re-exploring them for fresh possibilities. Some showed themselves to be most ingenious in novel applications of apparatus, in ways that had not occurred to the staff nor, indeed, to the designers.

It seemed to us, on occasions, that many pupils were catching up on missed play opportunities in their own childhoods. We came to recognize this as important and as a significant part of the scheme's success that they could feel free to do so without the presence of jeering and mocking 'mates'.

Similarly, pupils with reading difficulties had opportunity for practice at the level of their competence in its skills. The more successful introduced their interests and hobbies – the musician, singer, actor, the computer expert, the good draughtsperson or painter, whatever their particular interest, there was the opportunity to import it into the nursery. That gave us as tutors further opportunities to personalize our knowledge of them as people rather than as pupils.

Discussions with individuals and small groups, back at school, allowed us to give legitimacy to the varied responses we found among them. They helped each other to insights, afterwards, which had gone unremarked at the time of their experiencing. They often needed confirmation of this kind, that their responses, though different from those voiced by others, were within the normal and acceptable. Simply watching a pupil too deeply engrossed in an activity to have noticed one's entry into a room, provided many insights and revelations, indeed. To witness a reputedly 'hard man' display unexpected, uncharacteristic, tenderness to a child, or consoling the upset, were experiences well worth having for the tutor. Then to be asked, pleaded with, not to make any reference to what one had just seen 'when you get back to school, Sir', provided an ideal opportunity for the foundation of teacher–pupil confidence, for the future.

By such means, we discovered the significant influence on effort, behaviour and performance the presence or absence of his or her peers can have on a pupil. It is a salutary reminder of the pupil's private self and of the distinction it is necessary to make between that, often hidden, self and the public persona that school and peer-group demands from our pupils.

The opportunity to explore oneself outside of the usual terms of reference of peer-group and classroom, to discover and have the opportunity to exercise those characteristics and qualities of one's self which, at best, find only vicarious expression in the classrooms and group, is an aspect of educational provision we too often ignore or undervalue.

The lessons for the tutors

We are persuaded by our own experiences through these placements that we got to know our individual pupils far better than through many more hours of work with them in conventional lessons. The class/group lesson frequently reinforces the stereotypes usually attendant on pupil–pupil and pupil–teacher relationships. It puts constraints on, and often militates against, the kinds of self-exploration that maturing demands and that 'know thy self', as an ultimate educational aim, requires.

In a society and youth subculture where even the girls are required to be 'hard men', the kindlier, more tender feelings can be made to appear non-adaptive and inappropriate to survival and are often swept aside by the averaging effect of group norms.

That is not to minimize the importance of conformity. It does, though, raise the question of the improvement of the group standard and of the influence it brings to bear on individual perceptions of progress between conformity for 'safety's sake' where conduct is governed by a demanded and grudgingly given consent, and commitment by assent, where the self-knowing individual finds closer to full satisfaction without an identity-denying gulf between private person and public persona.

That statement of the problem of 'satisfaction in the context of other people's demands' we saw as central to the whole project. As we understood it, we were attempting to find strategies that would meet the needs of disaffected pupils in particular. It seemed sensible to assume that the atmosphere they found objectionable was present for all pupils, disaffected or not. We concluded, therefore, that the issue was not one of a relatively small number of disenchanted pupils for whom special and separate provision had to be made, but a situation where degrees of withdrawal from, underachievement within and disruptive behaviour toward what was traditionally provided, had to be countered on behalf of all the pupils.

That was why we chose to avoid the targeting of a select group and decided, instead, to devise a scheme which included all fourth- and fifth-year pupils. Thus, every boy and girl has a nursery placement at some point in the programme. We thought it best that the differing kinds and degrees of need, that the pupils had, were best met by universalizing circumstances because integration into the mainstream of the school was the ultimate goal, after all.

Another reason for our avoidance of a target group arose from our conviction, gained from an earlier initiative at the school, that such groups are at high risk of fulfilling the criteria that lead to their selection. They take on that identity and the peer-group pressures within it will strongly tend towards its reinforcement. Also, the boisterous, unco-operative pupil most likely to be chosen by a large number of agreeing staff for the overtness of his or her problem is not necessarily more in need of help than the quiet, withdrawn and underachieving pupil who might, thereby, get overlooked.

Add to those the chronic non-attenders whose longtime absence may categorize them as 'no real problem' and we have isolated at least three forms of disaffected behaviour. With such variety of pupil-need and with varying responses to existing curriculum provision, wherever the causes of disaffection may lie, the selective treatment of the more troublesome symptoms of it are unlikely to prove curative. Unless we see disaffection and disenchantment as a school problem, too, we stand little chance of banishing it as a pupil problem only.

When one discovers that one type of chronic non-attender rejects school because it is perceived to be a friendless place and/or experientially overwhelming in the amount of coping it demands for the unconfident, and that another type feels s/he has outgrown the need for it and is too mature for its 'childishness', we are forced to recognize that a single solution is inappropriate.

We are very conscious of the part our nursery placement scheme played in alerting us to the complexities of relationships within and to the variety of responses to a school as a social and learning environment. We now realise how very different may be the perceptions of the same place and people among those who have to function within it.

It was but one-sixth of the total of 'new' experiences the project made available to the pupils. All of them enabled pupils to view themselves in new contexts. The special feature of the nursery placement was that its demands confronted the individual pupil outside of the peer-group setting. Though at the outset, the educational need for this freedom from peers was based on a 'hunch' rather than on a well-formulated educational theory, for the insights it allowed us into our pupils as people and learners and ourselves as teachers, we do not regret following our hunch.

Since this was an experimental project and we were exploring strategic possibilities, we saw ourselves as learners. We were not, thereby, disowning previous years of teaching experience, but, rather, trying all that experience in a number of new contexts. Though the lessons to be learned were respectively different, we, like the pupil were entering new territory. True, we had more 'metaphors' from earlier experience by which to articulate comparisons than the pupils had from theirs. Overwhelmingly, by their responses, the pupils showed themselves worth any and all of the risks the contemplation of change first presented.

Adapting and consolidating

The six-activity programme is compulsory for all fourth year-pupils. In the fifth year, we allow freedom of choice within blocks of grouped activities and introduce an element of negotiation during that process. Our argument for this procedure is not only that of the logistics of organization. Without experience there can be no anticipation. Good choices are based on earlier knowledge and experience.

Some pupils resist, even with the compulsion. Oddly, almost perversely, 'the activity we are on now is the greatest', as one half-term succeeds another. A reminder that the pupil went on to enjoy the other activities similarly resisted, is usually persuasion enough. The more resistant are accompanied on their first visit. We know now that the nursery children will accomplish the task by taking command and showing the newcomer what is on offer. Even the hardest would feel churlish to resist further. It occurred to us somewhat later that much of this reluctance could be avoided by sending the pupils, whenever possible, back to their own former nurseries.

The best propagandists for the scheme are the pupils themselves. Having got to know and to win the trust of the influence-leaders among our own pupils through our meetings with them in the course of their placements, the most resistant can be referred to them. One of them openly professing favour – 'it's not going to be a bit like you think' – is usually recommendation enough.

The activities are now beyond the experimental stage. They

have been given a place in the school's core curriculum. The nursery placement, as with the other activities, has been accepted as a unit of credit by the Northern Examination Association. This has further enhanced it in the pupils' estimation as 'worth doing'.

We regard it as an essential part of our social and personal education programme. It contributes to a preparation for parenthood. It is as important to remind the girls as it is to persuade the boys that fathers are parents, too, when it comes to countering sex-stereotyping.

The community farm project

LESLIE HOWARD

In this project it is the school itself which creates an 'outside' environment.

Leslie Howard's curriculum report takes us through the process of development from 'rural studies' with a group of 'disaffected fifth-year boys' to the establishing of a community farm with plans for 'cheesemaking, tool repairing, crafts of various sorts' and plans to 'experiment with alternative power sources'.

The story is a very heartening one but it is worth noting a number of 'throw away lines' which indicate something of the commitment required and the difficulties overcome. The first point to be noted is the element of opportunism, 'there were, however, two grassed quadrangle areas of approximately one acre each' . . . 'eventually we secured thirteen acres of ground near the school'. Using the outside environment means making something of what is already there and it needs a particular quality of imagination in the teacher and a willingness to commit time and effort to negotiating with everybody from the school caretaker to the local council.

Although little is made of the issue, this account also illustrates the effects of disruptions to school routines. It is left to us to imagine the reactions of some of the staff when 'rabbits and chickens kept invading the staffroom'. There must also have been those who were disturbed by the very popularity of the course itself.

Finally, as with the other curriculum reports, it is worth noting what is said about the effects on pupils, both for what it indicates about their attitude to school in general and for what it tells us of what the project workers value in pupils and see as important developments.

When I first took over my present post, I inherited, along with the job, a large group of disaffected fifth-year boys, of whom, by this stage, very little was expected. Since we had two terms to 'get through', I knew that it was essential for me to find and establish a motivating strategy. The subject area that I was working in was rural studies, but there were no growing plots nor any animals in the school. There were, however, two grassed quadrangle areas of approximately one acre each, and these were not being utilized in any way, so we decided, as a group, to set about converting these into practical working areas. What we had in mind was the basis of a school farm – a project that caught the interest of the boys immediately, since most of their work to date had been classroom-based, and they liked the freedom of being able to work in the open air.

The range of skills that this project was to involve were endless. The boys had to begin by measuring out and removing all the turf from one of the areas, and then preparing the soil, ready for planting. The whole group was involved in researching the type of planting that would be suitable, what sorts of plants were available, what growing conditions were required and so on. The second quadrangle, we decided, would be used for keeping small animals in. One of the major tasks that this involved was designing and building a large pond. The boys carried this out on their own, including doing all the measuring, the working out of the amount of cement needed, and the actual digging out and building of the pond. All the landscaping and the fencing for the area was undertaken by the boys, which necessitated a great deal of planning and researching, apart from very heavy physical work. They needed to work out cubic capacity, areas, and some quite difficult equations. Where my skills were inadequate (which was very often), the students sought the help of other members of staff, who were always very supportive.

Once the basic area was completed, we took a trip to an agricultural auction, and bought some ducks, geese, chickens, and a peacock and peahen. The town-orientated boys thoroughly enjoyed the whole experience, and learned what they needed to know amazingly quickly. By this stage, they had established some credibility with staff, since they were no longer, on the whole, behaving as 'difficult' pupils, but were working with responsibility and a sense of self-importance. Other pupils, once they saw what was happening, wanted to join in to work on what was fast growing into a small farm. I was asked to expand the work, and insisted that if this were to happen, certain aims and objectives should be met. First the subject, and therefore the approach, had to have credibility. This could be achieved by opening the farm to all ability ranges, and to include girls as well. It would also be necessary to offer some final qualification. The project was to be offered as an option to all students.

Once accepted, the option take-up was overwhelming. Most of the third year included it as a first or second choice. It was decided to run three fourth-year groups, which required an additional teacher joining the scheme.

The farm began to develop in many directions – we acquired a much bigger collection of animals, including goats and pigs, and extended our crops to include wheat, corn, and a wide range of garden vegetables. Obviously this kind of work meant investing a great deal of trust in the students, who had to learn to take responsibility not only for their own actions, but also for animals in their care. The introduction of the animals into the school was transforming; for the boys, in particular, the care of animals gave them a chance to express a more caring side of their characters, without losing face. All the children became fiercely loyal about the farm – and therefore about their school – and despite all the warnings we had had about the inadvisability of having animals in the school, in case they were maltreated, our children treated them with enormous care, and were very protective about them. For those students who had become disaffected with education, the scheme gave them something in their school life to be proud of outside school, and there is no doubt that behaviour patterns in school improved significantly.

We were hampered by the lack of a greenhouse for the growing pots. Eventually, we located a very large greenhouse, 24 feet by 12 feet, and the students dismantled it, transported it by lorry from its original site, lifted the whole thing part by part over the school roof, and reassembled it, with immense skill, in the growing area. Finally, after electricity and water were connected, a new dimension was added to the school farm.

At this point it occurred to me, since the children were now full of stories about relatives who had some experience of either horticulture or of animal husbandry, that there was a wealth of expertise to be tapped for the project outside the school, so friends and relatives were invited to work with the children. This was fairly successful, and the adults who came in to help added a very important element to the whole project. Obviously, their presence modified the behaviour of the children, and links between school and parents were being forged, leading to a much greater understanding from both sides.

By this time there were some 130 students from the fourth and fifth years, and 180 students from the second and third years taking part. We were fast outgrowing our resources, and needed to see how and where we could expand. There had, of course, been problems on the way; the staff were sorely tried when rabbits and chickens kept invading the staff room, despite all our attempts to fence them in. The peacock kept flying out of the school and roosting in various parts of Wythenshawe, attracting a great deal of attention, and Faye, our goat, had to accompany me home in the holidays – which put something of a strain on my family! The animals were also very noisy, and as the classrooms surround the quadrangle, it did make teaching over the sounds of the geese and the cockerel rather difficult. On average, however, the good outweighed the bad, and what the students and school gained from having the farm there was worth the inconveniences.

I then began to look for some other land, away from the school, where local people could become fully involved in creating, with the children, a farm that would truly be a community amenity. A public meeting was held in Wythenshawe, and a committee was formed to help expand our school farm into the community. Eventually, we secured 13 acres of ground near the school, and development work began in earnest. We started by acquiring charitable status for the project – a very important factor. Since then, many groups have become involved, including our feeder schools (who were already enthusiastic visitors to the school farm, which again helped to make links between primary and secondary staff and pupils), the Health Authority, a Manpower Services Community programme for the unemployed, a YTS scheme, and a senior citizen's club. The school students still have a daily input into the farm, and work with or alongside a whole range of groups. Currently, we have plans to develop skills such as cheese-making, tool repairing, crafts of various sorts, and to experiment with alternative power sources.

Apart from the more obvious learning experiences gained from this project, what I think has been really significant has been the rise in self-esteem of the students involved, and the involvement of the parents and the community in a school-based activity. Because we have needed – and will continue to need – endless funds, we have arranged a lot of social activities, again including all three groups. Many of our parents now have a much clearer idea of what is going on in school, and feel more at ease about coming in and talking with the teachers (rather than being talked to). Equally, we, as teachers, have benefited enormously from the skills that the parents have been able to bring into the school, and from the greater understanding of the children and their families that the inclusion of the parents has been able to give to us. We are truly working in partnership, and if that could be extended to wider areas of the curriculum, which we hope will be a natural development, we cannot but benefit all round.

The other vital element is that the students are beginning to see the relevance of much of what they have learned in the classroom; they now know that they need mathematics if they are to carry out measuring and planning exercises; that they need to be able to write letters, and communicate easily with people if they want to be involved in a community scheme, and so on. I have referred to 'self-esteem' several times; Wythenshawe is an area of great social deprivation, with very few amenities, and a lot of economic hardship. Its distance from the city centre, and the problems of transport, mean that many people living there are experiencing a sense of isolation that culminates in low morale and a sense of worthlessness. When translated, in children, into apathy – a feeling that nothing can be done to change the circumstances in which they find themselves – this is very damaging. What this scheme has done, above all else, is to empower our students – to make them see that they can do something about the environment, that they can bring about change, and that, in fact, they have done so already.

Turkish Girls' Centre – Berlin

KRISTEL HAUTMANN

The Turkish community in West Germany, like immigrant communities the world over, tends to hold strongly to its cultural values and separate identity as a means of coping with the problems of living in a foreign land. The Turkish Girls' Centre in Berlin begins with the premise that such values must be 'respected'. If the tradition is that 'daughters must stay in the house except to go shopping and to go to school' then the centre must cater for girls only and must include 'training to enable them to do their domestic tasks more efficiently'. Here it is the community and the prevailing culture which demands a working environment, not in this case as an alternative to school but as an extension of school. The German school day begins earlier and finishes earlier than the school day in Britain and homework is expected of all pupils as a part of their normal working day.

It is worth noting the implied tensions between the overt western attempts to promote an 'equality culture' and a provision which, at least in part, seems to reinforce an 'inequality culture'.

The Turkish Girls' Centre has as one of its main purposes the meeting of two cultures, one a strand within Western culture which places a high value on 'women's liberation' and the other a culture which places a high value on male power to the extent that the women in the culture have their contacts and communication with the outside world mediated by the male (power) group. The neutral ground represented by the Centre offers some hope that the tensions associated with this meeting of cultures might at least be made more bearable. This does raise the whole issue, however, of school and home cultures and not just cultures associated with different racial origins.

This curriculum report should lead to questions about how cultural tensions of all kinds are resolved. As with the nursery placements report it may be necessary to get out of the school in order for the tensions to become apparent and for changed attitudes and adapted behaviour to become possible.

Elisi Evi, an informal drop-in centre, was set up to meet the special needs of young Turkish women and girls, living in the disadvantaged inner-city areas of Kreuzberg, Berlin. The centre is exclusively for young women, to accommodate the views of the local Turkish community. But it also provides a bridge to German society, culture and work, in support of our education and other services in the neighbourhood.

The Elisi Evi Resource Centre is part of a network of initiatives and projects set up in the Kreuzberg area as part of a programme of urban renewal and social, cultural and economic development.

Originally a typical working-class area of workshops and small firms near the centre of Berlin, Kreuzberg became isolated geographically by the division of the city by the Wall. Its population and economy declined. Many German families left the area, and Turkish families arrived in increasing numbers to settle in the old-fashioned flats, their children making up as many as 70 per cent of pupils in some schools. Many young people, German as well as immigrant, are faced with poverty, bad housing, and poor educational prospects mainly due to the lack of support on the part of their families, the poor vocational training facilities, and the high rate of youth unemployment. The Turkish community is predominantly from a rural, pre-industrial society, and attitudes to education generally, and that of girls in particular, are very traditional.

Many problems confront young women who arrive in Germany at the age of 15, 16 or 17, having just married a young migrant living in Berlin. The young man himself may have been pushed, sometimes even forced, by his family to marry a girl from his village, during the summer holiday.

These young women are removed from their own background and have never lived in a large town. They do not speak German, are usually not entitled to a work permit, and find themselves very isolated.

Elisi Evi aims to help Turkish girls and women develop their individual, cultural and social identity, by helping them to emerge from their traditional seclusion and find their way in German society and the world of vocational training. The aim is also to provide practical help including looking for jobs, housing advice, legal help and leisure activities.

The Centre is exclusively for girls and young women. This presented some problems with the other social services existing in the neighbourhood. But the Centre had to take account of the custom that in traditional Islamic Turkish families the wife and daughters must stay in the house, except to go shopping or to school, and may not meet other men except in their immediate family. An earlier attempt by a group of secondary school teachers to establish a support group for homework, for Turkish girls, had found families unwilling to let their daughters stay out after school hours.

The Centre could provide educational and language help for young girls, while respecting the concern of their parents, particularly the fathers by ensuring that its activities would be available only for girls. Moreover, to meet the common objection that the girls were too busy at home to be able to attend, the Centre undertook to include training to enable them to do their domestic tasks more efficiently, that is dressmaking, cooking, cleaning, and so on.

Elisi Evi provides extra help with school work and homework outside school hours; German courses and courses in writing in Turkish, designed to meet the needs of young women recently arrived from Turkey; practical and manual activities such as dress-making, which would enable the participants to earn some money themselves, cookery and home economics, weaving and tapestry. There are group discussions on questions such as health, nutrition, marital relations, childcare, German customs and so on. Personal advice and counselling are given. There are home visits, contacts with individual teachers and vocational trainers, discussions about personal problems; practical, residence permits, contacts with the administration.

Apart from the problems of financing and managing this kind of centre, those in charge have been mainly concerned with the difficulty of irregular attendance by the young women in the different activities, especially school-related work. They tend to be kept at home to do last minute tasks. The problem was compounded by the temporary move of the school to other premises.

An intermediary role was called for, on the part of Centre workers, to bridge the gap between the desire of the young Turkish girls to lead the same kind of life as their German girl friends and the educational philosophy of Islamic parents. There were some cases of young people running away from home, and even attempted suicide. The Centre's workers collaborated with the social services in trying to help resolve such problems.

Successes include: involvement in the Centre of girls forbidden by their families to go anywhere else; a number of pupils achieving certificates at school, helped by the Centre's school work support; the development of feelings of solidarity among the participants, especially as regards looking for work and a change of attitude on the part of participants and their husbands, especially about the education of their children.

General comments

We can point to some general issues raised by all the reports. There is a tension between 'school organization' and the sort of opportunism which supplies a particular type of educational need. The value of much of the out-of-school experience seems to lie in the very fact that it is 'not school' and that somehow the school 'culture' is suspended for a time. Schools have a vested interest in the routine. Without it there can be a quick descent into chaos. How is an appropriate balance to be managed between the need for flexibility in order to take advantage of the 'accidents' of the out-of-school environment and the need for coherence and accountability, and even such practical matters as health and safety?

Even where the experience is incorporated into the school week or the school year there are major organizational problems to be overcome. These include the need to find teacher time and commitment, the need to account for the time spent out of school, perhaps through some accreditation system, the need to reach agreement about goals with the adults other than teachers involved in the programme. Do we value these experiences enough to allocate resources to addressing these issues? These are issues which will not go away. Even the minimal examples published with the National Curriculum attainment targets refer to the use of the out-of-school environment: 'Planning an outing' (English Attainment Target AT1 Level 3); 'Investigate and design traffic lights and one-way systems for a city centre' (Maths AT1 Level 10); 'Children should study aspects of their local environment which have been affected by human activity . . . for example farming, industry, sewage disposal, mining and quarrying (Science programme of Study Key Stage 2). 'Contexts [situations in which design and technological activity takes place] should include the home, school, recreation, community, business and industry, beginning with those that are most familiar and progressing to contexts which are less familiar (Design and Technology Introduction to the programmes of study).

One of the purposes of offering out-of-school experiences is to allow society and the local community to influence the school, either through the nature of the experience itself or by offering a sort of meeting place where cultural values can be examined. Does this lead to a re-examination of school values and ways of operating? A number of the reports imply a cultural divide among the staff between those who are susceptible to such outside influences and those who are not. There are two claims which are worth further investigation.

The first is that improvements in behaviour out of school carries over into school behaviour. Is this a consistent and a lasting effect? The second is that schools restrict pupils to childish or 'schoolish' behaviour. If true, is this inevitable or are there ways of adapting school organization and expectations so that growing maturity is reflected more consistently in school behaviour?

4

Changing Time and Space

Individually negotiated timetables

DIANE KING

This curriculum report demonstrates an imaginative and positive way of mixed-ability teaching through meeting individual needs. It succeeded in raising educational achievement, re-engaging the interest of disaffected students and had an additional dimension of directly involving parents as equal partners with the school. The benefits of such involvement are numerous and reflect many of the concerns which have been voiced as reasons for the new Education Acts. The model for such a successful partnership as this is one which will need to continue, accepting the constraints of a centrally-determined curriculum.

The three examples of timetables provided are worth considering. They display how pupils with differing needs and abilities were able to negotiate timetable elements and, in a sense, could feel that they 'owned' their timetables. At the same time, it is important to note the amount of work which staff had to devote to selecting the students and to liaising with the local community.

In 1988 thirty-eight students from my school, a mixed, multi-racial inner city school, took part in a scheme that was originally piloted with eighteen students the previous year, which involved the students being able to individually negotiate their own time-tables for their final school year. This attempt to address the individual academic, personal and social needs of each student aimed to increase the students' self-esteem, their attendance at school and their commitment to courses. It was essential that the students involved in the group were mixed in terms of gender, race and ability to ensure that the group could not be accused of being a 'sin bin', a fear voiced by members of the community and parents.

The procedure by which students were chosen was extremely important. A team made up of the head of upper school, head of middle school, the Alternative Curriculum Strategies (ACS) co-ordinator and the head of learning support formed the selection panel, looking at recommendations from all the form tutors and teachers involved with fourth-year students, which effectively meant nearly all staff. The criteria used for recommendations were those students who were seen to be poor attenders; bright students who were seriously underachieving; students who had considerable difficulty in social situations and mixing with their peers and those students for whom a mainly examination-based curriculum was otherwise seen as inappropriate. The selection team was also very concerned that the group should reflect the school policies on race and gender.

After the often difficult and complex selection had taken place, the ACS co-ordinator visited the parents of the students selected to explain in detail to parents the advantages of the scheme being offered to the students. These visits took place usually in the students' homes which was important as the link between parents and schools can be very difficult and steeped in mistrust and confusion. This initial step helped to build the links on which the negotiations took place at the beginning of the academic year between the students, their parents and the ACS co-ordinator. Students were privately interviewed during the first week of the Autumn term. This allowed students a greater sense of control over the direction of their own learning and access to the 'machinery' of the timetable. They were better able to make informed choices and understand the potential and limitations of certain choices. Therefore they were able to make a commitment to a curriculum that had been drawn up with their consent.

The academic choices students were able to negotiate were within six areas: mainstream GCSE courses, options courses, Alternative Curriculum Strategies courses which were unit accredited, community placements, work experience and tutorials. The ACS courses were extremely wide ranging and varied. They included ACS unit accredited English and mathematics, assertiveness training, canoeing, ceramic jewellery, self-defence, music-making, pre-driving, small business projects, pre-school literature, rock climbing, carpentry, welding and many Further Education (FE) link courses, to mention a few.

During their community placements, the students were involved closely with local groups based in nurseries and centres for the elderly. Students within the home base group negotiated local-based work experience on a one day a week basis leading to a full week during the second term. During tutorial time students evaluate their curriculum and work through a self-assessment programme. Tutors also monitor the students progress in mainstream areas.

As the students' needs were very diverse, the outcome of the negotiations resulted in the content of the students' curriculum within the group being extremely varied. Some students followed a mainly mainstream examination-based curriculum with access to the ACS facilities offered within this system, while others followed a mainly ACS-based curriculum, and some students a balanced mixture of both. Therefore within the same year group each student had access to her or his own individual curriculum. Tables 4.1, 4.2, and 4.3 are examples of individual student's timetables.

Table 4.1 Student one

	Period 1	P2	P3	P4	P5
Mon	ACS English	ACS English tutorial		ACS activities cycle	
Tues	ACS maths	college craft skills		small business project/work experience	
Wed	College Links Courses		–	–	–
Thur	ACS maths	rural studies		ACS music project (making a record)	
Fri	Pre-school literature	ACS activities		career	college craft skills

Table 4.2 Student two

	P1	P2	P3	P4	P5
Mon	Maths	Science	English	ACS activities	
Tues	science	home and community GCSE		English	maths
Wed	maths	English	humanities		art
Thur	English	maths	art	science	humanities
Fri	humanities	ACS activities		careers	home and community

Table 4.3 Student three

	P1	P2	P3	P4	P5
Mon	English (ACS) ACS group doing GCSE Eng course		Tutorial	GCSE PE	
Tues	ACS maths		GCSE art	small business project and painting and decorating	
Wed	College Links Courses				
Thur	ACS maths		rural studies	ACS making music project (making a record)	
Fri	Pre-school literature		GCSE PE	careers	art

Student one (Table 4.1), a boy, has been receiving 'special needs' support since the first year. He is not following any GCSE courses, but is following some courses which involve unit accreditation by the Northern Examination Association. By contrast, student two (Table 4.2) is a very able student who has become disaffected to some extent. She is following a programme which is largely mainstream GCSE, but includes the ACS activities. In 1988 the activities cycle involved choices, lasting for six weeks, from short units on: toy making, word processing, Batik and screenprinting, ceramics, electronic music, outdoor pursuits, computers, technology, community activities, drama and predriving. This student would also be part of the same student group for early morning registration time and for events such as the residentials. Student three is following some mainstream GCSE courses, for example in PE and art. He is also following a GCSE English course, but is doing this as part of the ACS English work by negotiation with English staff.

It is difficult, of course, to get much sense from a timetable of precisely what sort of things may be happening. This report is primarily concerned with the negotiation of individual timetables, but it may be useful to briefly give the flavour of some of the work associated with just two courses, which student one and student three were following. The unit accredited course on pre-school literature in 1987–88 started with students looking at examples of pre-school literature. The group decided to produce their own booklet called 'Pelican Pam's Party'. This involved them in designing and printing work and developing the associated skills. Eventually, they took their booklet into local nursery schools to use and also found that several libraries in the area wished to purchase copies of the booklet. The ACS music project involved the group in the processes of fund raising, letter writing, music, lyrics, keyboard skills, recording techniques, video production, sleeve design, publicity, marketing and so on. As a project it illustrated very well how members of the local community can collaborate with students. In addition it led to a polished saleable final product, sold locally and heard on local radio. Both these courses were about ways of learning through being thoroughly involved. What they also did, however, was lead to a product in which students took pride, which boosted their self-esteem and belief in their own capacities.

During both years, and especially during the first year, students' attendance increased dramatically. Staff involved recognized the increased self-esteem and confidence that students showed. We also saw students' attitudes to their education change. They had greater expectations and actively contributed. One manifestation of this is the number of young people whose attendance in earlier years had been extremely low, now applying for places at FE college. Many students also frequently came back to school to visit students and teachers after they had left, the very same students who previously had voted very loudly with their feet!

International Women's Week

SUE BOTCHERBY

This curriculum report describes an occasion when both time and space is rearranged to allow for different activities focusing on the celebration of a particular theme. The benefits of this approach were that the planning and preparation time raised the awareness of both staff and students. Because the week involved a large number of external agencies, most of which were unknown to students, it afforded a large number of separate events which gelled into a common experience impossible to achieve if attempted in a series of short sessions over a long period of time.

It is increasingly common for some schools to suspend the timetable, either completely or in part, for a short period. The theme might be 'Industry Week' or 'International Women's Week' or 'Technology Week', but the learning opportunities involved can be very similar, where the normal constraints of forty or eighty minute slots disappear. When the school as a whole is involved, other boundaries can become blurred as well. Different age ranges who might rarely, if ever, meet in an educational setting, can on occasion be usefully brought together. Pupils and teachers who are routinely insulated by the conventional timetable can come into contact with one another. Clearly, such times in the life of a school might be viewed as potentially dangerous by some, people can become aware of how things might be different for more of the time; pupils can begin to recognize the possibility of change to what they may have viewed as immutable and set in stone.

International Women's Day is traditionally celebrated on 8 March in recognition of the struggles and achievements of women in their fight for equality. Manchester City Council has begun to recognize the importance of this day, and has extended this in giving over funds to enable a week long series of activities to take place. Our school is situated on the fringes of the City of Manchester. We are an 11–16, girls' comprehensive, with a number roll of approximately 1,000. In line with the commitment of Manchester City Council it was decided that we as a school would express our support of International Women's Week.

The initial idea for the week started with a senior teacher, and the bulk of planning germinated from a very small group of women. The ideas for the week were supported by senior management, though in all honesty there was not 100 per cent backing from all of the teaching staff. The planning for the events of the week needed to be very thorough, and involved a lot of administration and contact with outside agencies. The planning time involved was approximately two months. We also had a limited budget, and therefore we relied upon the goodwill and commitment of the people with whom we came into contact. Much thought was given to the balance of activities, and the need to spread them across the age range. A lot of activities meant changes of rooms, and there were many alterations to be made to the timetable that week. Gradually in the months of planning, many other staff members began to get involved, and as the week approached it had germinated into a whole school enterprise. The information to be disseminated to staff and pupils was complicated.

It should be made clear that the normal timetable was not suspended for the whole week, with between one and two days remaining timetabled as usual for a typical fourth year. Even here, however, there was an unwritten expectation that subject areas might follow the theme and this did take place in many areas.

For International Women's Week we adopted an open-ended cross-curricular approach, so that the focus was not subject-based. The theme of the week was to raise awareness of the position of girls and women in society with an emphasis on developing positive strategies to combat the negative effects of sexism. The week was dedicated in some form to this theme. Assemblies, exhibitions, displays, trips and a programme of events ensured that there was an awareness of the importance of this issue. Teachers and pupils actively contributed to the week, and a high level of involvement from external groups and individuals ensured that the environment for learning would not be traditionally teacher-centred. Given that the week was concerned with raising awareness rather than the acquisition of knowledge in a well-defined subject area, it was necessary for us to look closely at the types of activities on offer. We wanted the people involved in leading events to be facilitators for the pupils, rather than instructors. We wanted the week to be as active, and skills-based as possible in order to allow the girls to develop positive strategies for themselves. Most of all we hoped that the week would act as a series of stimuli in order to encourage the girls to ask questions.

Questions were asked, and issues raised in some of the discussion workshops. A women's health team facilitated a discussion on sexual harassment and rape. The workshop was for the benefit of the girls. They were not directed, corrected or assessed, but were allowed a comfortable environment in which to explore their attitudes and experiences of these two issues. Apparently the girls were far more forthcoming when a teacher was not in the room! 'It was good and interesting and would help young women who don't know about others' was one of the comments after the event. Two women from the equal opportunities unit facilitated a discussion on discrimination at work. This was particularly poignant to the fifth-year pupils at the time. The girls also managed to disentangle some views for themselves on the City Council in a situation which was not penetrated by the media.

An all day workshop allowed some of the older girls an insight into the use of basic video equipment. The day was to be almost entirely experiential; negotiable with the Seeing Red Collective running the workshop, and designed to encourage self-confidence. This was thought to be especially useful, as most girls in schools tend to see video equipment in an entirely passive situation. Some basic ideas and techniques were initially passed on to the girls involved. The small amount of equipment meant that it was necessary for them to co-operate effectively with one another. They decided for themselves how they were going to use the video camera, what effects they could achieve, and what the eventual end product would be. This they all did in small groups. They were given licence to experiment with what they could. Eventually they were able to view the fruits of their own endeavours, which they obviously found stimulating and enjoyable. The women who ran the workshop were pleased with the initiative displayed by the girls, who felt that this particular area of new technology had in some ways been demystified for them.

The issue of self-defence began to have a high profile in the week. Many girls stated during discussion that they would like to see it as part of the curriculum. A large number of girls betrayed their lack of confidence in themselves physically through discussion. They seemed to think that a basic knowledge of self-defence would enable them to 'fight back' at harassment or attack in an active, rather than passive, way. Not all of the girls agreed with this view, but they seemed genuinely interested in the possibility of learning some of the skills. A woman police constable led a discussion and showed some slides on self-defence. This was particularly relevant to her as she revealed that police women were not allowed to carry truncheons, and therefore relied on their handbags! This talk was complemented by a workshop led by a self-defence team. This consisted of a man and a woman, who had a more or less equal input into the afternoon. The fact that the woman was highly skilled, strong and extremely dextrous gave the girls a positive role model with whom to identify. They gave a superb demonstration of various simple and basic self-defence techniques, which did not require force but skill. All the girls involved participated actively, and learnt very quickly through imitation and trial and error. The girls themselves were amazed at how effective they could be without possessing incredible strength. They enjoyed this event tremendously, and some were inspired to follow it up in their own time as an interest.

The events already mentioned were for the older girls in school. Some first years took part in a voice training workshop which involved drama, singing and chanting. This was intended to stimulate them verbally, and to give them self-confidence. They worked in groups, with an emphasis on co-operation. The idea was to eliminate embarrassment, and to encourage them to express themselves freely (not to be quiet and demure as little girls should be). The workshop was physically very active, and was led by Rosie Fisher who specializes in this type of training. The girls learnt how to make different noises with their vocal chords; they chanted in unison, copied sounds, and followed one another in turn. After initial embarrassment and unease, most of them threw themselves into the workshop. Some of them felt sick after the breathing exercises; most of them laughed a lot, and they were all exhausted. It was a new experience for them, if a strange one, and some expressed interest to try some more.

An anti-sexist and anti-racist shadow puppet workshop was attended by various first and second years. The workshop was designed to undermine racist and sexist stereotypes. It was entirely experiential, and the ideas that the girls came up with grew out of making their own puppets, performing and discussion based on this. There were no chairs or desks involved, and in fact this workshop took place in our careers area in the entrance hall. The open plan aspect to this workshop permeated through a lot of our activities. Much of the week was open and on view to as many people as possible.

The workshop led by a community theatre group was perfect in that it undermined racist and sexist stereotypes in a fun way, which was perfectly pitched for this age group. The workshop was lively right from the beginning, and ensured that all the girls present took an active part. There was a creative element, which involved making puppets and putting on a show. The variation in activities was stimulating for the pupils, and they obviously grasped the quite difficult concept of stereotyping at their own level.

For staff and pupils alike, our contribution to International Women's Week led us to ask questions about ourselves and society. The fact that it was a week long concentrated effort lent it importance and pre-eminence. That is not to say that any of the week's activities or strategies for learning could not exist outside of this context. The context was important in its concentration on a theme. This theme was about raising awareness, which inevitably led us to look at skill-based activities rather than the passive acquisition of knowledge. The involvement of outside agencies and an attempted whole school approach allowed us to step aside from the teacher-centred situation. There were problems with the week, and it was by no means completely satisfactory. The usual problems of time, resources, the curriculum, group size, and so on tended to dictate what could be achieved. We would have liked to address the international perspective much more strongly. We do intend to involve ourselves in International Women's Weeks in the future, so that they become recognized and established. We hope to build on the experiences of this one, with particular reference to the feedback from pupils.

In the middle of the night

JORGEN LUND

This curriculum report, from Denmark, provides an illustration of the enthusiasm such initiatives can generate amongst young people. The educational value of such work was in terms of skills developed and knowledge acquired for both the young people directly involved and those younger students who benefited from the work produced. There was plenty of opportunity for the development of oral and written communication skills with the telephone calls to firms, the production of a booklet and taking on the role of teachers to younger students. Additional skills of research, planning, organizing and co-operative working with adults and peers were also developed. Equally important though, and something which is impossible to test, was the sheer enjoyment young people gained from this learning activity.

Two Danish teachers working with school leavers whose topic was the world of work had difficulty in finding suitable material for their groups. They started with a well-worn theme – the school. Using cameras and tape recorders they interviewed and recorded all the people whose lives impinged on the school, the cleaners, milkmen, postmen, members of the parents' council, youth workers and others.

The pupils were so enthusiastic about this experience that they often asked for it to be repeated. The teachers did not see much point in the idea but one day the pupils decided they would like to visit work places at night . . . the new theme became 'Nightwork'.

The objectives of the exercise were that the students should understand the problems associated with shift work, and gain direct experience of a society which works twenty-four hours per day. The project ran for five weeks, using all the lesson time in Danish and modern studies. There were two excursions.

In class the pupils brainstormed to generate ideas of places which might be visited. Where do people work at night? Twenty suggestions were given . . . the Carlsberg factory, the hospital, the fish market, the power station, the fire brigade, restaurants, the transport authority and so on. Each student chose one and then telephoned to make an appointment to arrange a visit. In spite of many disappointments they succeeded in getting enough positive replies to plan an excursion. Armed with a map of Copenhagen they planned the route:

10.00 p.m.	The casualty department at Hvidore hospital
11.00 p.m.	The goods station
Midnight	The police station at central railway station
1.00 a.m.	Vesterbro post office
2.00 a.m.	Soup at a restaurant
3.00 a.m.	Taxi headquarters
3.30 a.m.	The bus garage
5.00 a.m.	Breakfast in an all night café
6.00 a.m.	The meat market
7.00 a.m.	Home to bed!

In spite of 15 degrees of frost and deep snow, the excursion was a great success. Dressed in their warmest clothes, with lots of tea in the vacuum flasks, they walked as much as possible, caught the bus and took one taxi.

After a day's rest to catch up on sleep they started their follow-up. The focus of the follow-up for these young people, most of whom had some learning difficulties, was the production of a class reader for younger pupils. With guidelines, they wrote articles, composed a song, visited an advertising agency to discuss ways of laying-out the material, chose the photos they had taken, and produced the booklet.

Finally, the students became teachers as they took their booklet to the third year class, who were very interested and asked many questions. Later they were asked for autographs! They had become real authors. The booklet was then translated into English.

From this excursion, properly prepared and followed-up, many skills were learned: making appointments, using references, typewriting, map-reading, organizing an excursion timetable, writing articles and so on.

It is clear that the drastic change of environment had a variety of useful outcomes: the change of scene was exciting and motivating in its own right; students became involved in a variety of activities through which differing skills and understandings were acquired and developed; other audiences became linked to the experience, so that it did not remain an invisible excursion only known to those young people who went out in the middle of the night.

The Dublin Work Exploration Centre

KATHY AUGUST

Sometimes it is seen to be necessary to create an environment which specifically mirrors more adult working conditions. This report illustrates a common type of provision which can be found in great variety in all European countries. The purpose of such centres is to provide an experience which is somehow closer to the adult working world than school can ever be. In this case the centre has a variety of functions. The activity described here is a simulated work experience project which is a standard package offered to schools but it is set in the context of a great variety of other activities which means that there is a 'valuable social mix which young people benefit from while remaining in a small secure environment'. As in other curriculum reports, there is an emphasis on preparation and follow up with the consequent commitment of staff time.

Although there is considerable flexibility in the work of the centre, it is worth noting the evidence that links with schools have a strong 'routine' element; the work is 'tied to the school curriculum'; there are 'preparation', 'production', and 'post-production' components and although tasks are 'negotiated' with pupils, the negotiation takes place in the context of things that must be done, such as preparing the lunch.

The curriculum report details the activities which young people were engaged in and which provided opportunities for negotiation, planning, organizing, discharging responsibilities, oral and written communications, group work, social and personal development and the satisfaction of producing a finished article which was of benefit to others. It is often the lack of 'follow through' which frustrates young people and prevents them from seeing their education as a logical sequence but rather as a series of unrelated blocks of content. Both the Danish and Irish experiences set identifiable targets which were subject to review and evaluation by both the young people involved and their teachers. The weight of evidence accumulated from the experience of profiling and recording the achievement of young people supports the value of such reflection. Both curriculum reports demonstrate that opportunities for exciting and relevant curriculum innovation may be created without huge expense and long-term suspension of 'traditional' schooling.

Work experience and college link courses for upper secondary school students are now well established in many high schools. The Dublin Work Exploration Centre (WEC) combines the value of both of these but, because of its nature, gives an additional dimension to the students' experience.

The Dublin WEC was developed to support curriculum initia-

tive in a group of inner city schools aimed at developing young
people's social and vocational skills through practical learning.
However, the activities developed in the schools required
additional space and resourcing. Consequently space was offered
by Dublin's Vocational Education Committee to establish a large
multi-work exploration centre.

The Centre is situated in inner city Dublin and is housed in
part of a Georgian terrace some of which has been bought by
private householders. At the time of writing the area is a mixture
of part decaying, part newly-renovated buildings. The Centre
itself has nine main rooms, a woodwork/workshop area, a craft
room, a meeting room, a kitchen, office and two recreation rooms.
The Centre is run by the Dublin Curriculum Development Unit
and managed by a member of the Dublin Inner City Project
Team. A management committee, representing educational and
statutory Youth Service interests meets monthly and determines
overall policy. The Centre is staffed by an administrator, a full-
time woodwork teacher and part-time craft and computer studies
teachers. There is also a full-time teacher responsible for the
development of links between the Centre, local schools and the
community.

The Centre aims at providing a range of practical educational
activities and support for three main target groups of young
people: those still at school, those in Youth Clubs and Community Groups and those in 'out-of-school' education programmes. For these groups the following activities are offered:
work simulation with periods of up to a week in full-time simulated work conditions making products for sale; community service with young people supplying goods or services identified by
local community interests; personal and social development, in
which students are engaged in group work involving drama or
other creative activities; craft work such as silk screen painting,
soft toy making and basic woodwork; catering for either self or
a small group; vocational preparation in the form of practical
exercises in retail and reception work; local studies activities of
town trails, urban orienteering and local history, and finally
computers, with familiarization courses intended to provide basic
keyboard skills and build confidence. The Centre does not only
offer these courses, but also provides women's groups, night
classes, night clubs, groups from 'drop-in' centres and young,
unskilled, unqualified 18–25 year old women in their first jobs.
In addition, it provides work experience placements and offers
sheltered work to assist with the rehabilitation of people who
have been in long-term institutional care.

Consequently, there is a valuable social mix from which young people benefit while remaining in a small, secure environment. The WEC offers opportunities for induction into off-site learning and work experience for much younger students than those in the final year of schooling. It is a 'halfway house' between school and the FE link course. The 'safe' climate encourages both girls and boys to explore and experience non-traditional roles and work.

The Centre ensures that for young people from schools, the one week placement is tied into the school curriculum. This is achieved by having three phases to the placement. The first, the 'preparation component', involves a visit from one of the Centre's staff in which s/he meets the students and the member of staff who will accompany them on the placement. During this visit there will be some information given to the students and a discussion about what they would like to concentrate on doing in their placement. The product they will make is a result of negotiation with the community so as to respond to a particular community need.

The second phase, the 'production component' is the week's placement itself. During the week students are involved in making a product as efficiently as possible. The various tasks involved in the production are identified and allocated to students. In addition, each student has an individual task during the week and these are negotiated with them. These may include being responsible for making lunch on one day of the placement, taking care of the tools, organizing a recreational activity or keeping a record of the placement. A review session is held at the end of the day to ensure that everyone is coping with their individual tasks.

Finally, there is the third or 'post-production component'. This is when products are officially handed over to the charities or organizations identified earlier by the students. Schools usually make this into a social event, with the students' parents being invited and photographs being taken of the official 'handing over'. It is then the school's responsibility for any curriculum follow-up during this final phase.

During one year the Work Exploration Centre ran thirty projects for students from twenty-six schools, with forty-five young people being accommodated at any one time. Counting both school students and other users, approximately 650 people used the Centre, and, of these, 60 per cent were girls and young women. In the mutually supportive atmosphere created in the Centre, young people are encouraged to participate in their local community and to use what they have learned in identifying problems and solving them. As such, the opportunities and experiences offered by the WEC are felt to provide the young people with a practical education in citizenship.

The Open Learning environment

BERYL JACKSON

Post-16 colleges are increasingly making use of environments such as the one described in this report. In these colleges they can become a major part of the institution's educational provision, unlike the multi-skills bases in the Alternative Curriculum Strategies project referred to in Chapter 2. These multi-skills bases were at one time often marginalized within the school, as areas set aside for underachieving or lower-attaining pupils. Now, however, many schools are developing flexible resource bases with similar principles for all pupils. Open Learning environments, such as the one described here, can involve a much wider range of staff and students.

The author points clearly to the concern that students should learn to take responsibility for their own learning and that having one's own space and time implies responsibility. The report emphasizes the difficulties involved for both staff and students who are not accustomed to doing much else other than telling and being told. One danger is expecting too much of students too soon and the need for constant and carefully structured support is discussed, together with the importance of setting targets for students. At the same time, teachers have to learn not to intervene in traditional ways.

Certificate of Pre-vocational Education (CPVE) students at my post-16 community college operate in an Open Learning environment for at least half their week – this can be up to 13 hours. This 'environment' consists of the CPVE base and the Open Learning workshop each offering a different emphasis on learning styles. The base provides an unstructured space for informal group work, visiting speakers, discussions, video viewing, tutorial and profiling sessions. The Open Learning workshop has a less informal atmosphere but aims to achieve a relaxed, friendly and welcoming feel for all learners across the college.

The base is a large carpeted room with stackable and easy chairs, a few tables – low and high – cupboards for storing students' work, paper, glue, felt tips and the paperwork which all students need to structure their course. The emphasis is on informality and flexibility. We have learnt through experience that the base must be staffed at all times. Students lack the experience of being responsible for their own space, especially when there are over 100 users all wanting something different. Inevitably a small dominant group takes over, depriving the rest of the opportunity to work through some of the problems of communal living and decision making. They require the support of a co-ordinating adult and the structure of a student committee in order for everyone to have a voice in the way the base operates. What has proved enormously helpful is enabling the students to liaise and negotiate with the caretaker and cleaning staff in order to establish responsibilities and expectations. Nevertheless, we still have to live through weeks of 'mess' before students realize that having their own space implies certain responsibilities.

The workshop puts less emphasis on the social development of students and offers a more structured, less informal environment. Care has been taken in its design and furnishing to present a very pleasant, relaxed and comfortable atmosphere. It provides space for work tables, an informal area for profiling and guidance sessions, and a variety of equipment which includes six BBC computers, two Amstrad word processors, three Apricots, three Smith-Corona typewriters specifically for special needs students, four Brother electric typewriters, two cassette players and a variety of tapes and software. There are display shelves and filing cabinets full of Open Learning materials, that is self-teaching units or modules in a variety of subjects – typing, word processing, GCSE modules, A-level units, basic skills support and CPVE assignments. Students are expected to sign in at the reception desk and book any equipment they need. Support staff from different subject areas are timetabled to help if needed. CPVE staff are present to manage and profile their groups.

Great care has been taken in the messages conveyed by this environment. It was created to respond to the perceived need that students, ideally, should take responsibility for their own learning in order to meet the challenges of the adult world. The atmosphere conveys the assumption that 'adults' will be operating in it. Silence is not enforced, students come and go as they please, seeking help only if they need it. They are encouraged to help each other and consider the needs of other users. They can move around, discuss, take a break or browse through the materials. Ramps allow access for physically disabled students, and equipment has been modified for them where necessary. Students and staff can operate together at every level, working at their own pace in their own time.

The rationale behind the reallocation of resources which has allowed this development to flourish was a response to students' changing educational needs. Students need support in the transition from one system of learning to another, from a prescribed, directed, teacher-led system to flexible autonomous learning which enables people to exploit educational opportunities for the rest of their lives. The students themselves decide what they need or want to learn, and how and when to learn it. Some require support of mainstream courses, others a completely individualized programme.

Open Learning presents a resource which is in itself a major challenge to many students' ability to exploit it. The implications of self-awareness, self-motivation and time management are immense. Tutors were also challenged by the need to change their teaching styles – experiential learning for us. Our main problem was expecting too much of students too soon. We did not fully understand the nature of this transition from school to adult life which Open Learning is trying to address. How does a student, suddenly expected to operate in an unsheltered, nondirective environment learn to function independently? We have found the answer lies in constant and carefully structured support.

We have seen that the process of transition has to be managed and monitored in small – sometimes very small – stages, experience of success and building self-confidence being the constant aims. During induction the students are initiated into the idea of taking control of their own learning. They are offered increased choice, their decisions are respected, the effectiveness of those decisions discussed.

The initial assignments are negotiated individually or with a small group. At this stage there is minimum choice. We have learnt that achievability is crucial. What do the students, often anxious in a new situation, feel that they can cope with and succeed at? They must be able to feel that they can complete the assignment and evaluate how they worked within a time-span which is comfortable for them. One student may take half an hour, another may need 15 minute sessions over 2 hours on the way to planning in days or weeks. We have underestimated in the past the difficulty some students have in *accepting* their own pace. They are used to the arbitrary limitation of the school bell, the expectations of teachers and the competitiveness of peer groups. We have seen students overwhelmed, anxious and 'lost' and for them, those are the feelings associated with learning . . . to be avoided at all cost.

We quickly realized that the acquisition of time management

skills was central to effective use of Open Learning. Target setting and identifying long-term goals are a central theme of tutor support. If an experience is enjoyable, enhancing and enriching, students are likely to want to repeat it. This attitude to learning has to be established before students can make full use of this mode of learning.

A minority of young people can take an inordinately long time to make the necessary adjustments. A student from a sheltered special school background took one and a half terms to work through her resistance to taking responsibility for herself. Eventually she said 'I've got to grow up, haven't I?' This realization produced a major shift in her attitude, and her self-confidence and self-motivation have blossomed. Patience and faith in the process is required – students do respond but, quite rightly, in their own time.

Owning one's own education is risky – it not only means taking credit for the successes and building on them but acknowledging the mistakes and learning from those. The necessary self-esteem and self-confidence is clearly encouraged by constant assessment of achievement. All achievements, personal, social, academic or vocational, are recorded on the students' personal profile. This helps the students to assess their own strengths and weaknesses and enables them to make reasoned decisions about their needs, aspirations and ultimate goals. This process can often mark a change in direction. Open Learning can provide some of the experiences necessary to achieve some of those goals.

An immature student finding this 'Open Learning' difficult to cope with said 'Nobody tells you what to do', but began to experience the feeling of achievement through his assessment sessions. He was unaware that making decisions was a major achievement and was encouraged accordingly, the smallest decisions pointed to a developing skill. Again, he matured slowly, building his self-esteem to the point where he now feels comfortable in an adult environment. Open Learning has had a marked beneficial effect on such students, with little idea of their own personal and career potential. It can be difficult for staff to give students the time and space to work through this maturing process.

Students who begin to feel part of an environment which takes care to communicate respect for each individual and their needs begin to view themselves in a fresh, positive light. The student mentioned above, not unusually, saw himself for the first time as a 'learner' rather than a recipient of teaching. One student moved from 'I'm not really doing much, am I?' at the beginning of the year to 'I'm far more motivated than I was because I work when I want to on work I've chosen to do'. An A-level student who had changed from wanting to go into management to becoming a nurse, said 'You put as much or as little effort into it as you decide . . . if you fail, that's your fault . . . but you achieve your own goals, not somebody else's'.

Our attitude as tutors has had to change. We are handing control over to the students. We have to trust that students want to achieve their potential and will, once they have overcome their fear of failing. We have had to move away from the role of teacher, holder of knowledge, and expert to that of enabler, facilitator, managers and guides to resources. We have learnt not to say 'You ought' or 'You should', but 'What would be best', 'How can you achieve what you want?'. We negotiate assignments rather than instruct, we use time to reflect with the students on experience and help them evaluate it. We have become allies, partners and a resource for the individuals we manage. Above all, we have learnt that without acceptance, respect and trust, students will not develop the self-confidence to exploit resources.

The hardest part of our transition has been learning how not to intervene and allowing students to make their own mistakes and help them learn from them. In short, we are learning not to be the expert, always knowing what's best for the student, but to share the learning experience.

The trip
BRENDAN AGNEW

This report, written by a student teacher, points to both the problems and the learning opportunities which a major incentive for students can bring. The learning opportunities were opportunities for both the students and the teacher. Planning the trip at school involved students in organizing finance, insurance, travel, finding out about exchange rates, using the telephone and so forth. More generally, the students were given the responsibility for the major decisions and gained confidence in their abilities to make such decisions and see them lead to real outcomes. The author points to what he learnt, that these 'thick kids' could do such things; that power and responsibility could be shared within the classroom; how one major motivating and successful educational experience can, on occasion, transform an individual student's approach to schools. That there are risks involved, that teachers and other students can be 'let down' is also apparent in this study.

Although this report does not suggest that much structured 'debriefing' or 'follow-up' work was done, the writer details aspects of the work and the learning experiences which took place at school prior to the trip. In this there are parallels between this study and the approach to the Dublin Work Exploration Centre. The danger of 'trips' and 'visits' is where they are just that, involving little in the way of structured relationships to daily school life. Where, as is commonly the case, considerable time is allocated within the timetable to preparation and follow-up, such events can be powerful motivating and learning experiences for both students and teachers. In setting up tight relationships between in-school and out-of-school activities, the artificial boundaries between schools as 'proper' places for learning and the rest of the world can be broken down.

During my third term as a Post Graduate Certificate of Education (PGCE) student, I worked in an inner city Manchester school, which has been merged twice in four years, and now finds itself as a two-site school with all the problems that involves. Although one would expect the staff to be somewhat demoralized following a long period of industrial difficulties, mergers and reorganization, the general atmosphere among the staff is positive. The school's facilities are somewhat limited, with old buildings in need of a lot of work. However, from the school budget, money can usually be found, an important point for some aspects of the City and Guilds 365 course in which I was involved.

The 365 class has been established for a number of years, and a good framework has been established with a well-qualified teacher–leader, who has managed to develop a sound relationship of trust with the 365 group. They have a clear relationship of mutual respect, maturity and government by consent. This group is already used to being consulted about their course – and indeed are well aware of their rights to be consulted. They see themselves as young adults, but are also seen as young adults. It is an unfortunate characteristic of this group that they are basically what would have been called in the past, 'the fourth-year remedial group.' This tends to make non-involved staff see them as the 'thick kids' who are to be kept busy, out of the way, and good only to get to set the hall with chairs! I had the opportunity of getting to know this group in my teaching practice in the second term, when I had them for RE. At that time I found them undisciplined, rude and very difficult in the classroom. To me they seemed to represent the worst example of inner city youth hopelessness. There was no motivation to work – they had no jobs to go to! Absenteeism was a big problem – usually less

than half the class would be present on any one day. This caused
problems of continuity in lessons.

Hence it was with some apprehension I came to the 365 group.
However, I quickly realized that in this case I was dealing with
them in a new context. The Pre-vocational option, and the fact
that this project was not related to GCSE, book-based activity,
and that it was to have a pay-out at the end, changed the
dynamism in the group completely.

The project I went to the school intending to tackle, was
related to the need for profile reports. However, I was prevailed
upon by the 365 co-ordinator to consider arranging a residential
weekend, as he had promised such an activity some time previously. We discussed this together at some length, and came up
with the idea that it would be a weekend in London, as this was
what had been mooted by the class. Rather than have the whole
class making the arrangements, it was decided that I should
have a small group – but in best 365 style, they had to decide
who would be in the group. With these ideas in mind, we set off
to encounter the beast!

The class met and the idea of a residential weekend was
explained and the group was asked how they would like to
appoint a central working group, and to my horror they decided
to go on a draw method. This left so much to chance – what if
'she' were chosen, or worse still, if it were 'he'? In the end I was
landed with six boys – unfortunately no girls got the job, and I
feel this had some consequences later on – no girls went on the
trip, and this may have been because they were not involved in
arranging it. So, from a random selection, I was sent off with a
group of six to arrange a residential.

During our first meeting, the bomb-shell dropped, and I had
my first experience of being put-in-my-place! When it came to
the discussion on where the weekend was to be, there was a
debate within the group whether it would be Ireland or France
– a long way from London! When I tried to redirect the trip I
was told that they were organizing it, not me. From then on I
could only sit back and direct or answer questions, but they still
made the decisions. I could advise, but not dictate. By the end
of the meeting, they had decided that they were going to France,
and I could only follow.

We held a weekly meeting in the school, lasting two hours
every Thursday, with a variation if needed. During that time we
discussed what we had done, what we could do, and what we had
to do before the next meeting. Normally I chaired the meetings,
provided out-of-school notes for those who went off to town to

fetch information, and kept on the right side of the office staff when we needed a telephone line. The group were interested in what credit they were going to get for their work, so I provided a small booklet for them to fill in with reports of what they had done. This booklet was to be the basis of a 'Letter of Credit' which was to be written at the end of the exercise. My own log book gives an account of the type of jobs they did, and the nature of the results. As a guideline we used the City and Guilds programme on planning a residential visit – using the check list as a basis for jobs and tasks.

My log book and the students' mini-log books, with a copy of my Letter of Credit, which were typed on school note paper for the boys' files, show that the students set up and successfully worked their own 'small business'. They also took full responsibility for the finance, knowing that if they made a loss there would be no trip. This, to me, is an important feature – there have to be consequences for failure – otherwise some would have no incentive for success.

The exercise was to develop skill, knowledge and confidence, and each letter of credit shows those areas where a student showed his skill and knowledge, and I believe that all gained new confidence from the exercise, and all said that they felt they would be able to do it all again – this time without staff needing to supervise.

The students wrote the letter, booked the hostels, sent letters home to parents, met the headteacher, begged money from the deputy head, arranged the minibus, raised their own money, collected the fee of £14 per student, deposited the money in the bank, got a copy of Youth Hostel rules, found out the times of ferry departures to Boulogne, made a list of things for each student to bring along, arranged insurance, found out about travel documents to France, made enquiries about exchange rates, found the rate of exchange in the *Guardian*. They were ready to go.

We set off – eleven students and four staff at 10 a.m. on Friday 12 June. They had underestimated the length of the journey, and by the time we arrived in Dover they were a little irritable and needed time out. The first night in the Youth Hostel was a nightmare – for me. I was left in the room with the eleven boys, and they managed to talk until 4 a.m.

The journey, next day, was calm – from Folkestone to Boulogne. The weather was good, and the ferry was not crowded. When we arrived in Boulogne the students were given a booklet to write down those things which they noticed were different

from England. This was the idea of the co-ordinator, but I felt
that there had been enough learning in the trip itself without
giving workbooks. However, on this I was overruled.

The pupils had a long free day – from 11 a.m. until 5 p.m. They
stayed together in quite a bunch, which was understandable, as
it was, for most of them, the first visit out of Britain. When we
met back at 5 p.m. they seemed to have managed well – none
had starved, and all had made some purchases. The trip back
was uneventful – a sleepless night before, and a long day promised a quiet night in the Youth Hostel in Canterbury.

The Canterbury Youth Hostel provided much more comfort
than was available in Dover. We slept well. However, the next
morning the warden made a complaint that some of the students
had been smoking. This point had been made to them before we
left Manchester – that on school trips there was to be no smoking,
and that furthermore it was against the rules of the Youth Hostel
Association.

A return trip to Manchester via London had been planned,
and it was decided that the three involved would be taken
straight back to Manchester by car, while the others had their
eyes set on the sights of the capital. It was my unfortunate fate
to be given the job of driving directly to Manchester. This was
the only incident in what was otherwise a perfect weekend.

Looking back it seems important to consider what both the
students and I learned. First, those students who organized the
trip gained the experience of organizing such a trip. The staff
could have done it with only about one third the effort they had
to put into it – but the students would not have learned as much
as they did. For some of the students this was the first time they
had occasion to use a telephone for anything formal. A telephone
manner needs to be cultivated in order to get the information
one wants, and some headway was made in this field of skills.

For my money, the main gain was the confidence which those
pupils will have in the future. Not many of them would have
had the confidence to go abroad alone – certainly not before this
trip. Now they have done it, there is no reason why they cannot
and will not do it again. This in itself was an education. In
addition, the log books display a wide variety of more specific
learning experiences.

As for me, this was not the first time that I have taken a group
away for a weekend. My previous experience involved taking
groups from a special school for boys with behavioural problems.
In that situation I made all the arrangements, and the pupils fell
into my scheme of things. They came along as passive receivers of

the work which I had done. When this weekend was planned I approached it in the same vein. I did not really believe that the students could bring it off, and thought that they would need the staff to step in and do it for them, so I was surprised at the autonomy of the students. Each week I arrived at the school to find that they had pursued some initiative, and actually put it into action. They had the ability to think things out and to do something about it.

I believe that some conclusions can be drawn from the weekend about education through experience which is what pre-vocational education seems to me to be about. First, lazy students can be fired with enthusiasm if they are given an incentive. An example of this was one student who was noted for his constant inactivity, yet when the idea took him he put everything into it, and became the virtual organizer. His new-found activity has been noted by other teachers in other areas, and is the proof that motivation plays a large part in the learning process. This is just one example, the best example, but the same can be said about others in the working group.

A second element is that those who did the work got a lot more out of the trip than those who came along on the back of the work of others. The problem at Canterbury did not involve any of the students who had done all the hack work. The idea that if you work for it you will appreciate it more is what seemed to be the case. Those who did the work were not the best in terms of ability – they were chosen at random, but they were the most co-operative because they knew the work they had done, they had planned it and they were therefore prepared to make it a good weekend. To sum up – the more you put in, the more you get out.

Finally, I should note that I have learned a lot about students' abilities, and their skills. But the most important thing which has come out of this weekend is that it is possible to share power and responsibility in the classroom. I am also aware, however, that this comes in time, and cannot be granted without the building up of respect and trust. The two teachers from the school who came along on the trip have been with these students since they were first years, and they have done all the ground work which made my job easier. They have already developed trust with the 365 group. Despite this, they were still let down by three of the students, but I think it is important to say again that those three were not the students who had done the hard preparation, and perhaps they felt they could abuse the weekend – after all, it had cost them very little. I look forward to further activities of this type, where one can give students the chance to prove themselves – not in set exams, but by achievements, enthusiasm and success.

General comments

Students on individually negotiated timetables develop skills of time management and experience modes of learning, which are invaluable adult resources. Flexible learning modes are already available through community education, TVEI, Enterprise in Higher Education, and some forms of independent study at higher education level. There is a clear consensus about the need to develop flexibility, as a response to change in society, for example the pace of change in technology, increased life expectation, new patterns of organization in work and working practices. Such opportunities to develop flexibility in learners are at the leading edge of these necessary developments.

School buildings may be very limited in this respect, and may generate dependency behaviours which are not helpful in increasing self-direction as required for recurrent and life-long education.

Most of the ways of using alternative time and space also demand flexibility in working in a cross-curricular fashion. They can deliver aspects of programmes of study in, for example, citizenship which are far more real than standard time and space in school. An extended period of time at the Work Exploration Centre or elsewhere, for example, provides opportunity for applying and integrating skills, technical, interpersonal, and cognitive which may have been acquired in 'normal lessons'. The limitations, as well as the benefits, of single subject study become clearer to the young person, as skills are applied. In addition, the acquisition of further specialist skills appears to be necessary, as tasks make demands so that the interpretation of the experiences into 'normal subjects' provides further learning opportunities.

Curriculum managers have a fresh opportunity to consider where and how the requirements of the National Curriculum can be fulfilled. Periods of intense time, activities weeks, imersion experiences for foreign language, or applied science, can equally well offer opportunities to achieve attainment targets, and if these can become the student's own targets, planned realistically into the experience, so much the better.

PART II

Pupils' learning, teachers' learning and the quality of learning

5

Teachers and Learners

GORDON BADDELEY

There are, of course, clear advantages for effective teaching in
proper and sufficient resourcing, and in the provision of an
appropriate physical environment. There is also much to be said
in favour of giving the teachers and the schools more time to
plan, to think and to evaluate their professional provision. Yet
none of these advantages can be fully exploited if what goes on
in the learning itself is seen as boring, irrelevant, or threatening
– a set of perceptions which are perhaps as attributable to teachers as much as to pupils.

It is what happens between a teacher and the taught that
counts, and that, above all, is the responsibility of the individual
teacher. One remarkable result of the curriculum reports is the
extent to which teachers have found ways in which to interpret
theory into direct practice, to take risks based upon what they
really believe. In doing so, many have refined or reappraised
those beliefs, or even fully explicated them for the first time. The
community farm project (see Chapter 3) demonstrated how staff
perceptions of the worth of an activity can change with direct
experience and involvement following the freedom to think radically. It shows how release from the confines of the classroom,
into the wider community, changed the attitudes of pupils and
teachers, both to each other and to that which is to be learned.

In many of the curriculum reports, the experience has been
recognized by the teachers as releasing them from stereotypes of
expectation of pupil responses and behaviour. This recognition
was a direct result of the different tasks and responsibilities
offered and accepted by both teacher and learner. The divide
between the teacher and the taught has blurred into a middle
territory which can unselfconsciously be inhabited by all. The
world of school has therefore become one which contains three
countries – that of the learner, the teacher, and that place where,
for a time, all have become both. Moreover, the evidence of the
curriculum reports indicate that the countries of learner and

teacher are, for the most part, no longer the exclusive domain of one individual or group. There are significant and important moments when pupil is teacher, or when teacher is pupil, to the enhancement of the quality of learning and of relationships.

How does this come about – for it quite undeniably can come about. What are the characteristics which give distinction to this world of teaching and learning? The progression seems to lend itself to a visual presentation, and is summarized in Figure 5.1. It is with reference to this chart that the central issues of teaching and learning will be developed here.

Paul Light and Martin Glachan (1985), in their studies of people learning in a variety of contexts, have begun to produce evidence of the powerful influence upon learning of the process of negotiation. The activity of explaining, persuading, or simply of expressing views and attitudes, creates a depth of involvement in the shaping of learning, and a commitment to its outcomes, which is more readily recalled and reapplied. The TVEI and the CPVE programmes have made specific use of this factor in the organizational framework and in the required methodology of

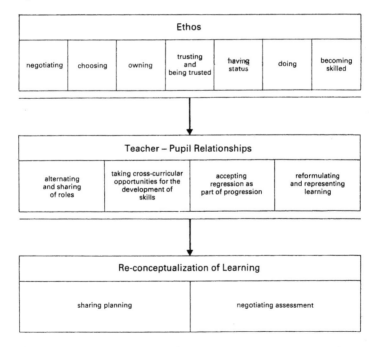

Figure 5.1 Issues of teaching and learning

the course presentation. Writers as diverse as James Britton (1970), Andrew Rothery (1981), Douglas Barnes (1976) and others have all reinforced this view in their work.

The curriculum report on the A-level teaching of *Mansfield Park* (see Chapter 2), reveals how none of the changes would have taken place at all had the teacher not responded to the early comments of the students and entered into what seems to have been a genuinely open discussion about alternative approaches to teaching and learning a novel. The breakdown of the A-level literature course into a series of modules created the opportunity, but the teacher was brave enough, in a publicly-examined course, to listen and respond to the views and attitudes of the students. Where the ideas and suggestions challenged her own expertise she sought, and found, expertise outside the school. The teacher says in her report that 'The actual process involved the students getting together as a whole group and deciding, firstly, what they thought were the most important aspects of the novel.'

The structured play project (see Chapter 2) was initiated by a 'period of intensive child/child, teacher/child and teacher/ teacher negotiation as to what each class should be responsible for.' In the report on individual timetables (see Chapter 4), the same principle was grasped with considerable commitment, enabling students to negotiate their own timetables for their final school year, and allowing them 'a greater sense of control over their own learning, and access to the "machinery" of the time-table'. This was not student choice, because free choice was not possible, the reasons for which the students themselves became aware. It was a process of listening and responding, of giving ground for given reasons, on the part of students and teachers. The effect, in the recorded experience of the teachers, was of markedly greater commitment, of positive changes in attitude and behaviour, of increases in attendance and in applications to FE, and of a pleasing tendency to return to visit their teachers after leaving school.

These examples illustrate that the principle can be valuable right across the educational spectrum. They also illustrate that it is not easy to apply. The teachers had to recognize and accept that negotiation is not persuasion, nor a subtle form of pupil-management towards pre-identified outcomes; it is a handing over of a significant element of decision making; it challenges the autocracy of the teacher, it creates partners in learning and it changes the student into a client.

A corollary of the principle of negotiation is the element of choice. Negotiation must enable the learner to make choices, as well as to understand and accept the choices made by others. This has important implications for the role of the teacher. What scope could, 'or should, be provided for the choice of content? How can one ensure that choices are informed choices? Is the learner necessarily the best equipped to make choices which may affect future opportunities? What about the freedom to make the wrong choice? The teacher in a report on running a multi-skills base (see Chapter 2) quotes one of the project workers as saying that 'the young people, in traditional classes, are not allowed to develop the sort of autonomy which they deserve as young adults, and which they need if they are to cope with an increasingly complex society.' The word 'autonomy' is an important one. It carries the assumption that the making of choices, and the readiness to be held accountable for them, is part of preparation for life. It is the outcome of the negotiation process, and suggests that consultation is a necessary and supportive element in the move towards the making and implementing of decisions. Moreover, students will need to accept that the decision is theirs, not somebody else's, without feeling that the decision isolates them from those who have been consulted. The teacher's role has therefore to become one of provider of information and resources, who helps the learner to work out what is possible, and its implications for future activity. The teacher has to follow through on student choice, giving it the possibility of becoming actuality.

In the creation of the Open Learning environment (see Chapter 4), the teachers observed the importance of non-intervention in a directive sense. The hardest part, they suggest, was to learn not to intervene, 'to allow students to make their own mistakes, and help them to learn from them'. In doing so, the teachers' previous perception of themselves as knowers and pupils as receivers of knowledge was fundamentally challenged, as were their concerns about classroom management and control. 'We negotiate assignments rather than instruct. . . . We have become allies, partners, and a resource for the individual we manage.'

There is, of course, a necessary tension between autonomy of choice and directed learning. In none of the curriculum reports does choosing take place in a vacuum. The environment within which choice takes place, and in many cases the parameters for choice, is established beforehand by the teachers. Students may, for example, negotiate their assignments, but be given no freedom to choose not to do them! Often, in the curriculum studies, teachers refer to themselves as managers, indicating an element of control and, in some instances, of manipulation of outcomes. The integrity of the approach lies in the reality of the choice, the freedom of contract drawn up by teacher and learner through which both accept areas within which there will be no choice, and the extent to which choices made relate to a student's own decisions and to the possibility of translating them into practice.

The question remains, is it ever desirable, or possible, for totally free choices to be made? Perhaps a number of teachers looking at the curriculum reports in this book will be motivated to move progressively nearer to effective structuring of choices within whole curriculum planning as they develop their own confidence and expertise. Perhaps there is a message here for teacher-trainers? Jan Turnbill (1986) writing about her work with primary children, identifies the art of 'conferencing', of enabling children to express, develop and reappraise their own ideas and intentions, as the most difficult and challenging aspect of her work. The combination of concern and respect; the need to help an individual to interrogate his or her own choice in a non-judgemental way; these are what makes this a skill of such great sophistication that it will need time and commitment for teachers to develop to the point where meaningful and responsible pupil choice becomes a real possibility.

Figure 5.1 (p. 104) uses the term 'Ethos' in an attempt to identify that atmosphere within a classroom, school or group, which suggests both informality and a sense of purpose. Rutter (1979), the HMI report *Ten Good Schools* (1977), the ORACLE research (Galton, Simon and Croll, 1980), all have noted and sought to define this. Teachers are well aware that those two characteristics can work destructively against each other. Informality can degenerate into the easy-going, the educationally diffuse and the directionless. Sense of purpose can be achieved at the price of overbearing discipline, close control, and externally-imposed goals. Indeed, the latter might well be attractive to many who feel that education is about these things – a notion reinforced by Kenneth Baker, then Minister of State for Education and Science, in his speech to the Conservative Party conference on 13 October 1988 in Brighton:

I want to see a return to traditional values in education and behaviour. . . . Children should learn their tables – and learn their tables by heart. . . . I want children to know about the main events in our history . . .

The emphasis here upon cognition, upon knowing things, and upon the traditional values, expresses a strong concern for outcomes – usually factual outcomes, and preferably testable ones. Many of the projects in this book arose out of realization among teachers and others of two educational facts: that such approaches as those implied above have not worked for the vast majority of our school children for the vast majority of their time; that being, doing and knowing were all bound up together in the process of learning itself. They accepted that *how* teachers teach is a primary determiner of how successfully learners learn. It is for this reason that teachers have been concerned with process, and it is why the notions of owning and trusting came to be such central features of this process. This has been, of course, a central concern within TVEI.

The learner seems, from the evidence of many of the case studies, to have taken over significant control of time, of the allocation and exploitation of space, of the process of decision making, and of the responsibility to make oneself accountable. The community farm project (see Chapter 3) involved 'a large group of disaffected fifth-year boys of whom, by this stage, very little was any longer expected.' Their involvement in researching what to plant, in designing and building the pond, was increased by the fact that 'the boys carried this out on their own'. The mathematics, notation skills and research skills which they had to use, was at least as impressive as the considerable physical labour. The teachers noted the increasing readiness to accept responsibility, the enthusiasm, and recognized the necessity to invest 'a great deal of trust' in the students. The success of the scheme is made evident by its expansion into an option, for all students, carrying a recognized qualification. Such work is far from easy. It demands resources of time, space and finance. Above all, it demands teacher commitment to motivate young people towards identifying their own goals, and trusting them to carry them through.

The nursery placements (see Chapter 3) are an outstanding example of trusting and being trusted. Both amusing and moving are the accounts of 'hard' pupils pleading with teachers not to tell about the 'uncharacteristic tenderness' they have displayed towards the nursery children. The whole project stands on the principle of trust. Young people are trusted with younger people and are expected to behave as teachers or caring adults with respect to them; school-based teachers are trusted not to use what they see and learn about the students in ways which would be interpreted by them as betrayal; nursery teachers are given the responsibility to treat the students with a set of expectations totally different from that which their previous school record might suggest.

Everything that has been noted so far contributes to one

common aim, to give status to the learner. The business studies project (Chapter 2) led to 'an increase in maturity, and the ability to exercise initiative in new and challenging situations.' The primary school child involved in structured play finds that the teacher is 'learning how to – alongside you really, things that you're learning' (Chapter 2). The pottery report (Chapter 2) refers to 'high expectations and high quality goods.' The multi-skills base report (Chapter 2) records 'feeling like part of a big family.' The college–school links course (Chapter 3) lists 'giving pupils student status while in the college' as a major element in the course's success. The community farm project (Chapter 3) records 'the rise in self-esteem of the students' as 'really significant.' The list could go on, a powerful accumulation of evidence to support the relationships between self-esteem and successful learning. It is not a new notion. Teachers, and writers such as John Holt (1971), Gerald Cortis (1977), David Holbrook (1964) and David Hargreaves (1984), have been fully aware of this for many years. What is perhaps new, is the uniformity with which the projects have, independently of each other, both endorsed this relationship and found ways of making it work.

Perhaps one of the most interesting pieces of evidence lies in the status achieved by those young people placed in the nursery schools, because this demonstrated dramatically the contrast between their achieved status and that of their pre-established public identity. The experience seems to have gone a long way towards releasing the inner personality of these young people into the public world, not least because in separating an individual from his or her peer group enables the development and expression of truly individual traits and values.

That all the projects set out to teach through practical activity, through direct experience and through simulation techniques is so obvious that it hardly needs comment. Yet it must be said that if self-esteem is at the heart of the outcomes of the work, then practical, experiential learning lies at the heart of the process itself. It is through deciding things and doing them that knowledge, skills and attitudes are developed. It operates at two levels, that of having an experience, and that of sharing an experience. The feeling of attainment is the sharper and more potent for being shared with others. The sense of self-esteem is the more valued for being reinforced by others. Every single project has been active. The students of *Mansfield Park* created a production; the Residential was characterized by discussions, productions and lively evaluations of their own work; the Danish teachers' project on 'Nightwork' combined an excursion with the production of a class reader for younger pupils; the junior and infant children's structured play simply took over the whole enterprise. Two features are perhaps worth a special mention. The first is the potency with which working for an audience seems to motivate the learner. As soon as the audience is extended beyond the teacher, and especially where it is extended downwards towards younger people, the momentum of activity seems to increase, including, quite importantly, the concern of the learner to raise his or her standards and to get it right. The second is the influence upon quality of motivation and outcomes of the involvement of non-teachers and non-pupils. The ethos is significantly changed where the world of learning embraces experts other than the teacher and non-experts other than the learner. It is as if those strange barriers between school and the real world are removed, and young people are able to bring the concerns of schooling to the wider community and share them.

A brief word is necessary about formal operational skills. The projects constantly provide opportunities for the acquisition and development of a wide range of skills, not least those of literacy and numeracy. A number of these projects took place in schools where such learning was seen to be primarily the responsibility of individual teachers in distinct areas of the timetable. Yet making opportunities pay off is the essence of the teacher's art. There are two main reasons why perhaps more attention should be given to exploiting the motivations and involvement of the young people even more towards the development of formal operational skills.

The first is simply precisely because they *are* more motivated and involved, and this has something to do with the fact that the practice of the skills are not ends in themselves, but means to other ends which are the more acceptable because the learner has been involved in identifying them. The second is a more pragmatic reason. If the approaches and strategies described in these projects are worthwhile, then they must be proved to be so, not only with reference to the criteria of the teachers themselves, but with reference also to the criteria used by others, however contrasting such criteria might be. Whatever the educationist might think of the skills and attitudes valued by others, it has to be recognized that those others may well have a profound and lasting influence upon the future of the young learner. In any case, a process which does not help the learner to read, write, speak and compute with skill and confidence is always going to be difficult to justify. The maths scheme shows how these concerns can be successfully combined, especially in the amount of literacy skill brought to bear upon the learning of mathematics. The business studies project successfully developed formal skills within an informal context, even though they gave up buying sets of books.

The opportunities are there in abundance, but it is necessary to structure them more carefully, and to raise their status within the context of experiential learning and National Curriculum planning. In a sense the 'constraint' of National Curriculum planning is a lever for having to consider these factors in a much more systematic and accountable manner.

The effect of these principles upon the quality of teacher–pupil relationships is quite remarkable. The fact that the teacher is no longer the automatic expert, but a fellow learner combines powerfully with the opportunities to choose the area of learning activity, and to represent what one has learned to another audience. The effect has been, through sharing the planning of work, collaborating in its execution, and open discussion of judgements at the point of assessment, to cause teachers to reconsider what it is to teach, and learners to re-evaluate what it is to learn.

Does it all matter? Does it make any difference in the long run? The direct experience of the teachers, pupils and others reported here constitutes a powerful affirmation that it does, and the research of Peter Mortimore *et al* (1988) reinforces this notion.

If this evidence is valid, then there is no longer a case for claiming that the influences of the home and the street are overwhelming; it is no longer satisfactory to use some of the seemingly constricting demands of the National Curriculum as a justification for the retention of methodologies that have a history of failure. In spite of the call for a return to 'traditional standards', there are clear opportunities both with the core and foundation subjects and the cross-curricular themes and dimensions to structure learning experiences so that they meet specific targets and yet retain the qualities of motivation and engagement which are features of these new methodologies. Indeed, the structure of attainment targets and levels could provide the broader reference and recognition that many 'alternative' schemes have lacked. It is easy to point to specific examples. The farm project would provide the context in which pupils come to 'know that plants require specific minerals for healthy growth' (science AT3 level 7) or that 'variation in living organisms has both genetic and environmental causes' (science AT4 level 6). In technology 'Pupils should be able to identify and state clearly needs and opportunities for design and technology activities through investigation of the contexts of home, school, recreation, community, business and industry' (technology AT1). Pupils are hardly likely to do this if the traditional classroom is the only learning environment available to schools.

When we add to the detail of the attainment targets the need to deliver cross-curricular themes and dimensions such as citizenship, the importance of opportunities to develop self-reliance, good judgement, effective decision-making and autonomy become self-evident. The case is there for exploiting the potentials of the National Curriculum, and of the home and of the environment in the structured individualization of learning, using practical, experiential strategies combined with expert supportive techniques.

6

Teachers Learning

JOHN COGHILL and ALAN GOODWIN

The case studies in Part I present, largely from teachers' perspectives, highlights of their experiences in attempting to involve pupils actively in their own learning. Moving from the traditional situation in which the teacher takes full responsibility for what is taught, to one in which pupils are expected to take their share of responsibility for what is learned, requires a substantial change in the teacher–pupil relationship. The when, where and, crucially, the how of teaching and learning may also change significantly if attention is switched from the needs of the teachers, the syllabus or the institution and focused on the learning needs of individual pupils in relation to statutory curriculum requirements.

There are striking parallels between the pupil developments outlined in the curriculum reports and the personal and professional development of the staff associated with them. Without exception, by some means or another, the teachers have been given the opportunity to experiment. They have been given the responsibility to identify problems and, working alongside colleagues and pupils, to seek solutions. Substantial evidence for their increased confidence, enthusiasm and competence to articulate their professionalism lies with the production of these reports. Although it cannot be proved, we would strongly suspect that prior to their involvement in the initiatives they describe, for some teachers at least, the presentation of such papers would have been unthinkable. They have become much more confident and adept at justifying and presenting their ideas. Clearly, having to explain to colleagues why there are rabbits and hens in the staff room must develop creative thinking, but unless there is a substantial and visible educational benefit, it is likely that such occurrences would hasten the end of the innovation! Teachers have had to take on very extended roles in negotiating with pupils, colleagues and the outside world.

Involvement in the range of initiatives described has been an almost continuous staff development experience for the teachers associated with them. The focus has been on learning by active engagement in problem solving which, for some teachers at least, has produced success and professional satisfaction beyond their best expectations. It is significant that there is little mention anywhere in the curriculum reports of traditional in-service training. Apart from a reference to the need for updating in new technology and to a teacher receiving in-school support from an adviser, the notion of staff development is not expressed explicitly. Yet the curriculum reports are strong examples of the personal and professional development of staff.

This may tell us a great deal about the needs of teachers. Certainly, many of the staff involved show themselves by their enthusiasm and commitment, to be as adaptable and willing to embrace change along with all its implications, provided that change is for the benefit of the young people with whom they work. They may well, however, never have reached the point at which they felt the confidence to embark upon innovation without supportive structures within their schools. Many of the initiatives have owed much to far-sighted decisions and no small amount of risk-taking at a senior level. Active learning can and often does generate movement, noise and relaxed relationships in a way which could be anathema to schools where good order, silent classes and autocratic discipline are the watchwords. Management support is, therefore, an important motivator, but even the greatest enthusiasm can wane if this support does not translate itself into more tangible resources. Materials, equipment and the facility to reorganize teaching areas are important but are nevertheless secondary to the most important resource of all, the allocation of staff time. Time to talk to pupils, time to plan with colleagues, time to develop materials, time to reflect and learn. This is all time which is so often denied to teachers but from which, in varying degrees, the teachers presenting these reports have benefited in terms of their own development. For many teachers, staff development time has meant occasional release to attend an externally provided course where the agenda, the content and the method are all prescribed for them. Directed time and staff days do at least offer the opportunity for teachers to engage in collaborative activities whose nature and content they are, theoretically at least, in a position to influence. This sense of 'ownership' of time and the staff development which can accrue are well illustrated by the curriculum reports in this book.

There are lessons to be learned here by those of us interested in providing in-service teacher education. Within a context of national imperatives it is crucial that the local issues and, consequently, the needs of teachers are increasingly defined by the teachers themselves. The providers of in-service training must, therefore, become responsive, flexible and supportive. Their role, like that of the teachers, is changing to that of a facilitator who can assist in the definition of problems, the search for solutions and their evaluation. The position of in-service providers as the experts with ready-made answers to all educational questions is no longer tenable, if indeed it ever was. There will always be, however, a demand from teachers to have the opportunity to extend and update knowledge and skills appropriate to their professional and personal needs. Content, particularly in the fields of new technology and the redefining of syllabuses as required, for example, by GCSE and by the National Curriculum, is constantly developing and staff need the knowledge and skills to keep pace. The pattern of course attendance has, however, changed significantly and it is now common practice for an individual to participate in in-service training as a step towards returning to school as a 'trained trainer' who will disseminate knowledge and skills to colleagues in-house. In our view, this model too is somewhat outdated. It is innovatory, recorded and shared practices by teachers in their own schools which the curriculum reports capture.

The period of TRIST (TVEI-Related In-service Training), funded by the then Manpower Services Commission between August 1985 and March 1987, was notable for its emphasis on the methodology of teaching and training rather than content. Although specifically concerned with staff development for the 14–19 curriculum, TRIST was seen from the beginning as a full pilot for the LEA Training Grants Scheme (more commonly known as GRIST) which was to follow in April 1987. The cycle of needs identification, design, implementation, evaluation and review became formalized. Staff development was seen as a collaborative process with the clients having the opportunity to make an input at all stages of the cycle. The principles of TVEI became embodied in the approaches to training which were largely participative, active and experiential and based on teamwork. Skills linked to resource-based learning, team teaching, negotiation, counselling and profiling are increasingly interwoven with the knowledge-based content of staff development provision associated with the National Curriculum. As schools move towards coherent development plans, there is a real opportunity for relating curriculum content and teaching and learning methods in association with a concern for learning environments.

The examples of activity-based learning in this book show that, from the staff development perspective, perhaps the major advantage of shifting the physical environment or reorganizing the timetable is that this requires a renegotiation of the stereotypical, sometimes antagonistic, relationship between teacher and pupil. Teachers, both individually and in teams, can co-operate with their pupils, a co-operation which can begin to extend even into the assessment programme. This is not to suggest that, in the past, teachers have not co-operated with pupils, nor even that encouragement of active involvement of pupils in their curriculum has been discouraged. It is only recently, however, that the idea of real negotiation with pupils and giving them responsibility for aspects of their own curriculum has been legitimized within the context of relatively high status developments.

For all pupils and teachers, such experiences can stimulate a positive relationship which legitimates a partnership in learning and, for many, re-establishes the value of much of the conventional curriculum. Thus, it seems appropriate that attempts can be made to present the National Curriculum with diverse activities and experiences. We hope that this exploration of the staff development aspects of a variety of teaching and learning environments is not over-optimistic. Certainly, the level of commitment required from the teacher is recognized and should not be underestimated.

It is clear that most of the curriculum reports derive from 'experimental' educational developments on a pilot scale. Inevitably, this tends to engage the enthusiast in the process of problem solving. The fact that the teacher does not have pre-set answers almost requires that pupils are engaged in the process of defining and solving the problems, and this seems to be a vital component in developing the co-operative relationship. Keeping this aspect alive and institutionalized for subsequent cohorts of pupils and disseminating the ideas and techniques to other teachers are major challenges for the future in the context of whole curriculum planning. Once the teacher has experienced a successful project, visit or activity, there is a danger that this will be imposed on subsequent pupil groups without their being realistically engaged in the process of decision making, planning and implementation which is where the real learning lies. A real experience becomes reduced to the level of a worksheet and it is virtually impossible for pupils to negotiate when working their way through a worksheet.

Similarly, it is not reasonable to expect all teachers to engage in the pioneering stages of changing the learning environment. Others must be able to learn from the experiences and errors of the experimenters, but true personal and professional development requires that they too must engage in the process. Following another's recipe without the certainty that it is fully appropriate for the problem in hand is unlikely to lead to active learning and could be completely counter-productive. The absolute requirement is for whole staff development plans which allow for the sharing of effective individual staff development experience. Useful advice is beginning to emerge here, for example the DES advice on *Planning for School Development* (Hargreaves *et al*, 1989).

The examples in this book and the references made to the trends in approaches to staff development are hopeful signs for the future. They take on even greater significance with the Education Reform Act and the plans contained within it for greater centralization of curriculum and assessment, and what to some appears a much more rigid approach to the management and organization of schools. One initial response to the Act has been to suspect that opportunities for flexibility and negotiation will inevitably diminish. This may turn out to be the case but it is not inevitable. The Training Agency is involved in a new series of pilot programmes aimed at 'The management of more effective learning' to explore ways in which information technology might be used to allow teachers and learners to manage individual, negotiated, learning programmes. TVEI is supporting a number of 'Flexible Learning' projects and individual action planning is being written into contracts for TVEI extension. This illustrates the considerable interest in managing the complex task of interrelating elements of individual design and purpose and statutory curriculum requirements.

With self-management, schools will in fact, as managers of the learning environment for their pupils, have considerable control over the 'how' of learning and, through relationships with those they teach, will have a prime responsibility to motivate them in terms of the 'why'.

7

Assessing Learning

MIKE COCKETT

Pigs and pence

As a currency, pigs have some advantages over pence. They have an intrinsic value and given reasonable care they increase and multiply. In an enclosed society a barter system can sort out problems of relative value and a marketplace economy thrives.

Pigs have two great disadvantages, however, their lack of portability and their mortality. The transfer to a purely symbolic currency reduces bartering time and increases transfer both of money and goods. The marketplace expands from the village to the whole country and eventually the whole world.

This chapter considers the relationship between educational activity seen as having intrinsic value, and the need for a standard accreditation which aims to give value through the symbols of grades and levels – between pigs and pence.

In some cultures pigs and other animals came to be used as symbols of wealth, at least in the first instance, because they were 'wealth', just as the gold coin was once worth its own weight in gold. The development of coinage with no intrinsic value happened in stages until we reached the present stage of intrinsically worthless bits of metal and paper symbolically representing wealth, whether in gold or in pigs.

In our society, knowledge and skills are wealth or at least the raw material from which wealth is created, and schooling is part of the process by which this raw material may be extracted. To understand some of the developments taking place in this field, particularly as a result of the 1988 Education Reform Act, it is important to recognize that the educational currency system is part way between pigs and pence. There is a concern for the intrinsic value of learning and that it should be 'relevant' to the needs of society, for example, or that the development of the individual abilities should be paramount. There is another and sometimes competing concern that the learning should be 'valued', that it should have some recognized spending power in the educational and jobs marketplace.

Pupils and parents recognize the intrinsic value of certain activities such as putting on plays or doing community work, but question their place in the curriculum because they do not lead to examinations or improved grades. The profitability and, to a certain extent, the longevity of the examination grades often outweigh the immediate satisfaction of the curriculum as it is experienced.

The curriculum reports illustrate in a variety of ways the tensions which arise when trying to resolve competing claims on school time, on the one hand for that which is perceived as being intrinsically valuable, particularly to individual pupils, and on the other, to that which has a value ascribed to it by external authorities.

This chapter aims to explore some of the complex issues raised as schools try to work on both the intrinsic and the symbolic value of the outcomes of educational processes.

Task Group on Assessment and Testing

The agenda for this debate was set by the report of the Task Group on Assessment and Testing (TGAT), and before looking at assessment in a variety of learning environments a short commentary on the report is necessary.

The secretary of state's terms of reference for TGAT revealed the complex of cultural and functional purposes to be fulfilled by the new system. The main purpose was 'to show what a pupil has learnt and mastered, so as to enable teachers and parents to ensure that he or she is making adequate progress and to inform decisions about the next step.' However, two other purposes were also identified. Summative purposes by which each pupil's attainments can be 'compared with attainment targets for each subject' and 'publicising and evaluating the work of the education service.' (Black, 1988: para. 7.)

The report itself was more specific about the purposes of assessment. They were to be:

formative, so that the positive achievements of a pupil may be recognized and discussed, and the appropriate next steps may be planned
diagnostic, through which learning difficulties may be scrutinized and classified so that appropriate remedial help and guidance can be provided

summative, for the recording of the overall achievement of a pupil in a
systematic way
evaluative, by means of which some aspects of the work of a school, an
LEA or other discrete part of the educational service can be assessed
and/or reported upon.

(ibid: para. 23)

The terms of reference did not recognize any problem in recon-
ciling these various purposes and the report itself resolved a
number of contradictions by representing both learning and
assessment as a straight line graph with standard variations built
in to represent the various ability levels at each 'key stage'.
Without going further into the details of the TGAT report, it
can be seen that one major purpose behind the programme is to
make the pig redundant. The attainment targets will become
the gold standard against which educational progress will be
measured for individual pupils and which will be the basis for
measuring the educational wealth creation of teachers and teaching establishments.

Both of these might be legitimate aims as long as the gold
rush doesn't destroy the rest of the economy. The problem is
that it begs a number of crucial quesitrons:

– Can learning be represented as a straight line or, for that matter any
sort of consistently upward curve?
– Is the learning 'curve' the same for all people?
– Is the only difference between the most able and the least able the
speed at which they learn?
– Is learning along similar pathways for all types of knowing, for example appreciation of a poem and an understanding of a scientific experiment?
– Does learning take place along similar pathways regardless of the
method of learning?

It would be quite easy to extend the list.

There are also questions which have been raised about the use
that will be made of these results. The marketplace imagery of
this chapter has been chosen deliberately, since it reflects the
prevailing climate. Many people are concerned that the results
will be used, not only to assess performance against agreed indicators, but to 'sell' local authorities, schools and even individual
pupils. The danger of such a process is that market forces will
reduce education to a lowest common educational denominator
and that, in spite of the strictures, particularly in the supplemen-
tary TGAT reports, the curriculum will be reduced to that which
is assessable and many of the human values represented by the
work reported in this book will be lost.

The crucial point about these questions is that we do not know the answers. We have some hints and plenty of anecdotes which suggest that the neat picture so clearly desired by some politicians is a fantasy, but our knowledge of how human beings learn is still extremely limited. Given that such knowledge is limited, it does not follow that there should not be a structure of teaching, learning, assessment and reporting, only that the methods must be recognized as strictly limited and subject to modification in the light of the actual complexities of human development. The moderation procedures recommended in the report provide some mechanism for this sort of adjustment. It is to be hoped that they survive once the exercise has been costed.

There was one recommendation in the TGAT report which is crucial to the concerns of this book. It is worth quoting the full recommendation:

We recommend that the national system should employ tests for which a wide range of modes of presentation, operation and response should be used so that each may be valid in relation to the attainment targets assessed. These particular tests should be called 'standard assessment tasks' and they should be so designed that flexibility of form and use is allowed wherever this can be consistent with national comparability of results

(ibid: para. 50)

The rest of this chapter considers what can be learnt about assessment, its effects, the concerns of teachers and flexibility in setting assessment tasks.

Environments for assessment

One of the recurrent themes in the various curriculum reports is the revelation of qualities in young people which sometimes even they did not suspect that they had. The nursery placements curriculum report (Chapter 3) is typical of the way the new 'environment' can reveal qualities and abilities hitherto unsuspected. Similar comments are made in relation to the rural studies development (Chapter 3) and the links courses (Chapter 3). The pupils seems to 'gain in maturity'. They surprise their teachers with their 'autonomy' or their new motivation. Perhaps the most graphic example is the pupil who, although once noted for his laziness and inactivity became the 'vital organizer' for their trip to France (Chapter 4).

This emphasizes one of the major issues in assessment; the

means by which skills, knowledge, abilities, achievements, and so on are to be revealed. The tendency is to assume that only learning which can be assessed in certain ways is valid.

Indeed, these curriculum reports themselves show this concern. Many of the activities are alternatives to the 'standard' curriculum and in order for them to become accepted as standard themselves they must somehow be accredited. The 'link' programme (Chapter 3) shows this most clearly but the same concern is also shown in the A-level English programme (Chapter 2) where the students themselves were faced with the challenge from other A-level students and teachers. They were torn between following patterns of work which seemed to lead effectively to 'good grades' and those which seemed intrinsically interesting. The teacher felt constrained to work only within the normal time constraints for the topic and to reassure students that their examination performance was not being put at risk. Although it is presented as an aside, the teacher's comment that the work on *Mansfield Park* produced the best grades in the mock examination for these students is a crucial one. It is very doubtful if the experiment would have been allowed to continue if the results had been worse.

In this example, as in a number of others, validation and assessment are seen as necessary to offer status to the activity but they are not at the heart of the teachers' concerns. Indeed a number illustrate the impossibility of assessing in any sort of comparative way, the performance of the students. It is literally the accidents of the various circumstances which produce the desired learning. It is the unpredictability and the lack of comparability which is at the heart of the exercise. In the A-level English example (Chapter 2), answering questions in an examination is contrasted with answering questions from an audience at the end of a performance. The first can be prepared for with 'notes from the teacher', the second was much less predictable and therefore revealed qualities which could not have been observed so easily by the examiner.

The clear message from these examples is that in order for a wide range of human abilities and human learning to be assessed, it must be assessed and observed in a wide range of contexts. The danger still represented by the National Assessment and Testing programme is that it will, for reasons of cost or comparability, restrict the environments for assessment to those which are in some way standardized. In short, what counts as a 'learning environment' must be a standardized 'testing environment'.

Motivation and measurability

This tension between the standard and the unexpected or unpredictable also has a bearing on another main theme which runs
through the curriculum reports – the improvement in motivation
in the pupils as they become involved. The argument is that
improvement in motivation must eventually lead to an improvement in performance in a variety of fields. Some of the curriculum
reports comment that 'other teachers noticed the improvement'.
This illustrates the concern of the teachers to show some positive
effect on ordinary lessons. The problem lies in demonstrating to
the sceptic that such improvements are real and lasting.

A common objection to new schemes aimed at improving
motivation is that they simply teach pupils that it is their right
to be entertained, that they should not have to work at things
to be successful. The real world, objectors will say, is as much
about getting through the routine and boring tasks as it is about
engaging in the interesting and entertaining.

There is an important issue here. In effect, examination systems are a sort of postponed satisfaction. The argument is that
success in examinations opens up the world, allowing for a
greater choice and ultimately greater satisfaction in life. This
does not just apply to the obvious matters of gaining recognized
qualifications in order to get a better job, but also to such areas
as the arts, where the development of technique may require
long hours of practice and the negotiation of a number of hurdles
such as graded examinations in music or auditions or compe-
titions. The problem is, as any parent who has persuaded their
children to keep up their piano practice will know, that the
ultimate goal is not always sufficient as a driving force for the
young learner. They need to be kept at it with a combination of
routine and encouragement.

The pupils who have greatest difficulty in maintaining their
efforts are those who receive least in terms of adult support. This
can be for a variety of reasons. It may be that the adults in the
family simply do not believe that the system has any value for
them. They may have no experience of what is required to
achieve standards in many fields of work. Their energies may be
directed elsewhere, for instance into a family business. There
may be cultural factors which make it difficult for individuals to
appear to be accepting 'the system'. The net effect is that pursuit
of the immediate goals may militate against the sort of educational achievement represented by traditional examination success.

This is an additional reason why many of the writers of the curriculum reports are concerned to justify what they are doing, not only in terms of the motivation of pupils as shown in improved attitudes, attendance, and so on, but also in terms of improvement in the standard measured outcomes. One of the challenges which the National Curriculum is going to present to all teachers who believe in the variety of learning experiences presented here is how they can extend this work in the context of achievement measured against attainment targets, and reported at ages 7, 11, 14 and 16.

Chickens and eggs

It seems more correct to make assessment follow curriculum change rather than the other way round. In practice, it seems that the opposite is very often the case. This can in part be explained by the basic premise underlying this chapter, that we cannot consider educational outcomes only in terms of amounts of growth or learning. They have a symbolic value ascribed to them by our culture, which is more powerful than the intrinsic worth perceived by individuals. Failure to recognize the power of this symbolic value has undermined many excellent curriculum development projects. On the other hand, changes in the value system itself can produce startling curriculum change in a very short period of time. The best example of this is illustrated in the development of the business and information studies GCSE (Chapter 2). Of course, the curriculum development work had to be done first, but the impulse which has moved many business education teachers has not been the quality of the curriculum but the fact that it leads to a high status GCSE. The multi-skills business studies environment described was designed to suit the curriculum, but it is the fact that the assessment structure includes portfolios, individual assignments, mini enterprise, and so on which ensures its survival. This point is reinforced by the HMI report on the introduction of GCSE:

There has been considerable enrichment of the curriculum in years 4 and 5 through more broadly-based subjects which draw on a wider range of skills and concepts than in the past. The increased opportunities for groupwork and for pupils to take responsibility for their own learning have led to the development of skills which are more relevant to what is likely to be expected of young people when they leave school and take on further training and employment.

(DES, 1988: p. 16)

Production methods

The new Education Act leaves one territory still firmly in the hands of teachers and that is the choice of appropriate teaching method. It is difficult to know what to make of the reasons for this. It is, of course, a wonderful 'escape clause.' Any failure of the National Curriculum becomes the fault of teachers using inappropriate methods. Whatever the reason, it is based on a fundamental misconception that content and method can be separated. A pupil who has followed the business and information studies course (Chapter 2) may demonstrate the same knowledge of computers as a pupil who has followed a formal course in computer literacy. She or he will, however, have learnt a great deal more, not least the sort of effective working knowledge which comes from using things like computers as a means to an end and not an end in themselves.

On the subject of assessment, the curriculum reports provide evidence for the enhancement of learning when there is a regular feedback to pupils of information about their achievements. This seems to be a common perception as true of the maths class (Chapter 2) as it is of the college links courses (Chapter 3).

It is because changes in examination systems are so powerful and that what is learned depends so much on how it is taught that we need to pay close attention to the intention and eventually the practice of assessment and recording in the National Curriculum.

Market forces

The National Curriculum and associated testing and reporting procedures are an exercise in standardization. Such standardization, it is reasonably argued, is necessary if pupils, parents, local authorities and the nation as a whole are to have some way of assessing the effectiveness of our collective and individual investment in education. The secretary of state's responses to the maths and the science working party documents show clearly this concern with that which can be standardized and therefore compared. Taken to an extreme, such concern is absurd. It would place common experience and common learning above all individual differences for the sake of maintaining the value of the common currency. If such a strategy were possible, we would have to imagine generations of children whose educational market stalls, when laid out, would all sell identical goods, the only differences being the amount on sale.

The debate has moved on and the present secretary of state in his speech to the Society of Education Officers in January 1990 has recognized the absurdity of too great a standardization, at least in the upper secondary school. What had seemed like a prescription has now become a 'broad framework' for assessment at key stage 4 and although GCSE is to be 'the principal means of certification at key stage 4 it is not going to be the only means. For some, this raises the spectre of second class examinations for the less able. They fear a return to a system which divides pupils at an early stage into those taking high-status and those taking low-status examinations. To argue this way is to miss the opportunity now presented. The fact is that GCSE is a second-class examination for the less able. Examine the entry requirements for courses or employment post-16. How many will accept GCSE grades less than 'C'? In practice, only grades above 'C' are of much use in the educational and career marketplace. There are already signs that in spite of the perceived improvement in the intrinsic value of GCSE courses, significant numbers of pupils are dropping out of the courses early because they realize that their grades are not going to qualify them for anything when they leave school.

The National Curriculum offers an important opportunity to provide a range of qualifications and associated routes for progression. Because they are all linked to the same system of programmes of study, attainment targets and levels will not require or imply a division between the educational haves and have nots. The qualifications may represent differences in modes or contexts of learning and in methods of assessment but common criteria would allow 'rates of exchange' to be negotiated.

The fact is that attempts to give value to education by establishing common criteria for assessment and accreditation will have little effect on attainment and motivation if the resulting grade or certificate cannot be 'cashed in' on entry to the next phase of education, training or employment.

Breadth and balance

A truly healthy marketplace must be concerned as much with variety and individuality as it is with the common and the standard.

There are a number of ways in which such individuality can be recognized within an assessment and reporting system. There are those examinations which test particular skills or interests such as in music or modern languages. This is familiar territory and it allows for individual preferences and talents to be developed.

More recently we have seen the development of 'records of achievement' and 'unit credit' systems which have as one of their express purposes the accreditation, or at least the recognition of individual achievement. These systems are encountering two sorts of difficulty. The first is the familiar one of 'value'. Pupils, parents, teachers and employers all want to know whether the record of achievement or the unit of accreditation will count for anything in the world beyond school. Employers want answers to their recruitment and selection questions. For pupils the questions may relate to career choice or course entry. To say that they have a unique record of their individual abilities and achievements does not seem to be enough – they want comparative standards.

The second group of problems relates to the task of recording itself. Here we are close to some of the questions posed at the beginning of this chapter – who knows what any individual learns from any particular experience? The residential course provides a good example. There is potential for a great variety of learning; about how to be a member of a team, about taking the initiative, about cooking and cleaning, about how other people see you, about managing away from home, about leading or being led, about taking responsibility for your own behaviour. All these are 'written in' as the potential of the experience, but who knows who has learned what? Sometimes it is not even the pupils themselves. A variety of methods are used to try to distil the essence of such experiences. They include personal reviews by pupils, group discussions, reviews with a teacher or tutor and the provision of 'evidence' in a variety of written visual and oral forms. All these methods are very time consuming and they remain imperfect, leading to further questions about the value of using limited time in such activities.

Ironically, the world of industry and commerce, which although seems to be asking for comparative standards, also asks for precisely those qualities which are developed by such experiences; leadership, initiative, enterprise, flexibility, mobility and team work. It is not true that there is a consistent call from industry for a 'return' to a knowledge and skill-based system. Robert Reid, Chairman of Shell UK, at the North of England Education Conference in January presented a very different view of the needs of industry. 'In our recruits' he said 'we are not looking for knowledge – we are looking for mastery of the processes by which knowledge can be acquired and a maturity and sympathy gained from exposure to the mainstream of intellectual thought.'

The great danger of the new systems is that in attempting to make the education system subject to market forces it ends up devaluing the goods available. What is missing at the moment is any balancing factor which will stop schools, teachers, parents and others recognizing worth only in the educational 'currency value' and not in the essential individuality of their children and the positive value in our educational culture and traditions. The pressure to publish results, to think in terms of 'value added' as children progress through the system can surely have some benefit in raising base standards – but the desire for measurability, for standardization, must be tempered by the recognition of the uniqueness of each individual and the *immeasurable* value of education.

8

Pupils' Judgements

DAVID HUSTLER

Introduction

Interviewer: If you could choose again, would you choose the 'Alternative'?

Jason: Yes, I would choose it again. Because I know how good it is and it's better than normal school, I mean, like they look in the classroom, and people think they are not learning nothing, you are learning all the time, you know what I mean, because you are going out and going to Old People Homes, you are learning what life's like with the old people, like we was going out and organizing bingo for the old people, helping them in and out of their cars and doing for them, and you are just feeling that you are working out of doors, and it is giving you more confidence for like when you have left school. Like in normal lessons just writing, reading, having a break, having your dinner, going back, writing, reading all the time, you know what I mean.

The curriculum reports in this book are written by teachers. They convey a sense of pupil enthusiasm, but we need more than this to get at pupils' judgements. Several curriculum reports stemmed from work in Manchester LEA's Alternative Curriculum Strategies project. This chapter draws on part of the formal evaluation of that project – the part which focused on pupils' views, pupils like Jason.

There have, of course, over the last few years, been a large number of studies with an interest in pupil perspectives on teachers and schools (Hammersley and Woods, 1984). In addition several studies have discussed pupil experience of and reactions to curriculum innovation (Burgess, 1983; Evans and Davies, 1985). Of special interest in this book is just how pupils could make sense of their schooling. How could it be 'school' and 'not school'? In brief, the question is what sort of knowledge of teachers and schools were these pupils working with and how did their experience of an alternative curriculum relate to this?

The pupil comments used in this chapter come from a series of tape-recorded interviews, usually of about a half-hour's duration, with 70 pupils who were in an original sample, in 1983, of whom 50 were followed through to May 1986. The observations came from those 90 per cent of ex-pupils who said that, given their time again, they would choose such an alternative curriculum. Many of these pupils made comments such as the following:

'If I was in school I wouldn't have done the work . . . on the course there is more opportunity to do what you'd like in lessons.'
'They are doing lessons and we're not really doing lessons, because, well, we're doing lessons but in a different sort of way.'
'It's not like school . . . you don't want to wag school now because you don't know what you'll be missing.'
'It's not like normally, stuck at a desk in a classroom.'

Both during the project and afterwards, pupils seemed to have a problem when describing what their alternative curriculum was and how it was different from their previous experience of schooling, or their experience during other parts of the week. The problem was in finding the appropriate words: it was school but it was not school, they were teachers but not like teachers, we had lessons but not normal lessons. The same pupils seemed to have little difficulty in describing what their first three years at school had been like. This was, in fact, how most pupils described their alternative curriculum: in terms of what it was *not*. It was clearly not like 'ordinary school' and 'everyone knows what schools and teachers are like'.

Although 'everyone knows . . . ', the comments in the following sections do serve to highlight, at times quite dramatically, the type of knowledge of schools and teachers that these pupils are working with. This chapter, therefore, serves to provide a characterization of what 'normal school' is like, at least for many pupils. The comments are also used here in an attempt to get some sense of the major ways in which their alternative curriculum seemed to differ for these pupils and what they thought about it. The viewpoints are presented in three sections; 'lessons', 'teachers', and 'learning'. Although each set of pupils' comments is followed by a brief discussion, the aim is to provide sufficient material for readers to make their own judgements. A crude conclusion to this section could be that the comments suggest overall that 'it was school but it wasn't' and the next sections explore some of the details of how this could be so.

Lessons

In this section the comments are presented under recurring themes which emerged from the interviews. Each theme is presented in terms of comments which seemed to focus on what took place prior to, or outside of, the alternative curriculum, followed by comments more concerned with what took place during the alternative.

Writing and sitting

(a) 'Before you just sat down with a book and pen and wrote'
'They're just sat in classrooms writing'
'It was just writing on the board . . . especially in years 1–3 because that's all you ever do'
'In mainstream it's all writing'
'Normally you're stuck at a desk in a classroom'

(b) 'You learn more doing it than just writing about it'
'You didn't have to sit at a desk all the time'
'You're not beind a desk as much'
'It's good because it's not always writing'
'You don't just sit in the classroom and talk and write'
'You can sit down when you want to'
'You're allowed to move about'
'You can get up and walk about if you feel like it'
'You can make a drink when you want to'
'It's practical instead of writing all the time'

At least two issues seem to emerge from looking at these comments. First, the pupils seem to be working with a view of what normal school and normal classrooms are like in terms of what you do there, you sit, at a desk, and you write. That's part of life as usual in the classroom. However, it's not that you don't do such things in 'the alternative', rather you don't do them as much, all the time, always. You don't 'just' sit at a desk and write, and for these pupils that seems to represent quite a difference and quite a powerful way of communicating something distinctive about the project. Readers will, of course, be reminded here of many of the descriptions in the curriculum reports, as well as the discussions of principles such as choice and autonomy in Chapter 5.

Second, in the alternative curriculum project it seems as if you are not stuck at the desk. In fact you can get up if you want to, you can move about, you can even make a drink. You can walk about if you feel like it. You can even sit down when you want to. To be able to get up when you feel like it points, then, to a type of schooling which is pretty different. Being able to sit down when you want to suggests that there's something strange about these teachers, perhaps they are not 'normal' teachers.

Sameness

(a) 'It was always just the same, boring'
     'The first three years were all the same . . . same sorts of teachers, same sorts of lessons'
     'It was really boring, going slow, same lessons'
      Jason: Like in normal lessons just writing, reading, having a break, having your dinner, going back, writing, reading, all the time, you know what I mean.

(b) 'You didn't have set lessons'
     'It was changing continually'
     'You have to go to see what's going to happen'
     'It's a great break from the normal monotony of lessons'
     'It broke the week up . . . a refreshing change'

'Boring' is one of the words pupils use most often to describe school, and we are only beginning to get an understanding of just why it is so important for pupils to be able to 'have a laugh' (Woods, 1976). When you ask pupils to explain why it's boring, a common reaction is to look at you as if you are a fool; it's so obvious but fools may need the obvious, the taken-for-granted facts of life, explained to them. It's the 'sameness' of it all.

This idea of 'sameness', which pupils use or presume knowledge of to point to the nature of their school experience, seems to have a number of features to it in these comments. It's the 'same teachers' and the 'same lessons'. More generally, the pupils know only too well how the whole curriculum package is put together: there are lessons and bells and breaks and lunch and lessons and bells and breaks and lunch, and Tuesday is this and Friday is that. Jason certainly knows this. What pupils seem to be using this knowledge to point to is not so much that their alternative curriculum experience was different from this, but rather that life during the project contained differences. A problem with sameness presumably is that you know what is going to happen – it's 'always the same'. In the alternative curriculum it was unpredictable, you 'didn't know what you'd be missing'.

As a slight aside there is one sort of comment which occurs quite often: 'You have to go to see what's going to happen' and ' . . . you don't want to wag school because you don't know what you'll be missing'. These comments reinforce the argument that 'unpredictability' rather than 'variety' was an important difference about the project, important enough to not even want to 'wag it'. The aside is speculation as to what makes for such unpredictability. The inference which we might draw from Chapter 5 is that 'negotiation' may well have really got off the ground in a variety of ways. The more negotiation, the less there is predictability is a possible interpretation. There are, however, other plausible inferences. Whatever the inference, the implication for teachers that they might attempt to build unpredictability into schooling is quite thought provoking, particularly given some of the less thoughtful ways in which National Curriculum planning can be approached!

Doing 'what you are told'

(a) 'In classrooms we felt treated like little babies'
'It was always do this and do that'
'You couldn't put forward your own views'
'It was always being shoved down your neck'

(b) 'You weren't pushed into anything . . . hardly wagged it'
'In all other lessons it's the teacher that makes the lesson but in this you make the lesson'
'It gives you more of a chance to learn yourself'
'You could take your own time to finish things'

The comments relating to (a) are the least revealing of any presented so far in this chapter – we know this, pupils know this, interviewers know this, everybody knows it. Accepting this makes it not too surprising that quite a common reply to the question 'What was the best thing about it?' was the answer (similar to Jason's reply): 'The best thing about it was having a say in what you wanted to do.' A reply like this does a powerful job in terms of spotlighting the alternative curriculum as being different.

The comments in (b) above suggest that things are a bit different here, but the pupils seemed to value them highly; making the lessons, taking their own time, not being pushed into anything. Only one other issue will be touched on here and it's that raised by the last comment: 'You could take your own time to finish things'. It could be argued that through their talk in classrooms, teachers commonly display their ownership of time and that this is one aspect of their power in the classroom. Comments such as 'Do that in your own time' are fairly familiar examples. In several of the project schools, pupils had base rooms of the sort referred to in the curriculum report on the multi-skills base (Chapter 2). They clearly regarded these as, at least in part, their territory. To have a stake in the ownership of lesson time, as well as a stake in the ownership of space, points to a fairly unconventional sort of schooling in terms of the knowledge of schooling that most people share.

Teachers

The comments here are presented differently from those of the previous section, there being four groups of pupil comments. The first three groups: (a), (b) and (c), it is suggested, point to three slightly different aspects of what these pupils, and perhaps many others, 'know' concerning teachers. The pupils seem to make particular use of these three factors when describing their teachers as rather different. The fourth group (d) relates to pupil comments about that difference.

(a) *Not so 'nowty'*: 'If you mess about the teacher doesn't get mad'. 'Teachers used to get on my nerves'. 'Teachers are not getting on your back so much'. 'The teachers were nowty . . . always nagging'.

(b) *They learnt to talk*: 'Teachers explained things to you more . . . before they used to just walk away'. 'Teachers talk to you more'. 'They learnt to talk to you . . . they had a different attitude'.

(c) *Dead polite*: 'Teachers took more notice of you . . . like an individual'. 'Treated like an adult . . . dead polite'. 'You were treated more as a person . . . and asked to make your own decisions'. 'Now they talk to you like a grown person'.

For any teachers reading this, what does the word 'teacher' seem to mean for these pupils? Approximately as follows: 'teachers nag, get mad and get on your nerves; teachers don't know how to talk to you, don't explain things much, and keep on walking away; teachers don't treat you as if you were a person, let alone a grown person, and they are not polite'. No matter what curriculum content emerges with the National Curriculum, many pupils are not likely to learn effectively if they view most of their teachers like this.

The comments in (b) above are interesting in the sense that conventional wisdom states that teachers talk too much. The three extracts here are similar to many other comments which appear to be utilizing a different aspect of what 'anyone knows' about teacher talk. This is that teachers talk 'at you' rather than to you or with you; that teachers talk but don't explain things much through their talk; that teachers don't really know how to talk to pupils or haven't the inclination or the time. The way that they talk is what makes project teachers different. The comments remind us that conventionally, pupils are members of school classes and are treated as such. Being a member of a 'class' provides a working identity, which for the teacher handling a class and for the pupils recognizing themselves as members of that class, may subordinate or exclude other identities; such as being an 'individual,' 'a person,' 'like an adult'. It is interesting that only very rarely did pupils use the word 'classroom' when describing their project experience.

Pupils still used the word 'teacher', however, but seemed unsure about its use when describing the Alternative Curriculum strategies project.

(d) *They changed a bit*: 'They were like friends rather than teachers'. 'In normal school there doesn't seem to be much trust. When teachers are out of school they are very different people, human beings not robots sent to get on your nerves'. 'Half the teachers just go to teach and that's it . . . they're nowty, just want to teach and go mad. Some others are there to get on with people too'. 'Before ACS teachers were just teachers, but then they changed a bit'. 'He was brilliant; not like a teacher'.

Just as there is a teacher aphorism to the effect that 'school would be a great place if it weren't for the pupils', there are countless descriptions of teachers as the enemy from the pupils' point of view. At the same time, several people have noted references by pupils to particular teachers as being 'great' or 'like a friend' and not like a teacher. Most of these pupils refer to the project teachers more generally as being 'not like teachers'

and this is where there may be links with worries some pupils
had about what they were learning.

Learning

a   'It gives you more of a chance to learn yourself'
b   'We were learning all sorts . . . but we should have had some more
    formal lessons'
c   'We could have had more ordinary learning in the morning and ACS
    in the afternoon'
d   ' . . . might have learnt more if the teachers had been stricter'.
e   'It was learning things but not normal learning'.
f   'We should have had a bit more ordinary work . . . like maths and
    English'.
g   'You were learning through doing it'.
h   'The teachers were great, not like teachers . . . you didn't learn too
    much'.

Jason: 'Because I know how good it is and it's better than normal school,
I mean, like they look in the classroom and people think they are
not learning nothing, you are learning all the time, you know what I
mean . . . '

One of the remarkable features of many of the interviews was
a kind of urgent insistence by many pupils that they *were* learning
and that they had learnt all sorts of things during the project.
The reasons for this insistence are not really an issue here, though
it is possible to point to a variety of possibilities. It might be
argued, for example, that for several pupils this insistence was
fostered through opposition to the reactions of other pupils and
other teachers. The project generated certain comments from
outsiders to the project, which lived on in the memory of pupils.
Two examples from non-involved teachers were 'Get back to
your Wendy House' and 'Do you expect to get an O-level in tea-
brewing'. Comments like these seemed to place an onus on project pupils to look for the ways in which learning was taking
place and to look for a vocabulary through which they could
express this.

Another argument might rest on what was almost the sense
of surprise about their own abilities, when pupils spoke at length
about a particular skill they had mastered. For several, the surprise was not only to do with their own capacities, but also to
do with a recognition that you could 'learn' in settings which
were far removed from traditional school life. This language is,
of course, much more familiar in secondary schools now than it

was at the start of the ACS project: it is the language of 'learning through doing', of 'experiential learning', of 'activity-based learning', of 'problem-based learning', and so on, and the earlier curriculum reports made extensive use of such approaches.

Yet, even for those pupils who expressed with the most urgency the ways in which learning took place, this was commonly laced with comments such as (b), (c), (d) and (f) above. For some pupils, the absence of a lesson clearly marked maths or English troubled them, even though many were able at other points in interviews to comment on how pleased they were with their progress in these areas. Other pupils, although strongly welcoming the different relationships with teachers, also expressed a need for teachers to be a bit stricter. Many pupils felt they should have had some more 'formal' or 'proper' lessons, yet the same pupils eulogized about the project as being informal and different from normal lessons.

An interesting viewpoint regarding the flavour of many responses comes from one of the project evaluators commenting on interviews from one school: 'The problem which seemed to lurk beneath the text of their responses was how to informalize learning without losing the concept of learning as serious, disciplined and structured'. The same point must hold for schools as they move to develop their National Curriculum planning. The opportunity must not be lost to develop a whole curriculum approach which is disciplined and structured, and obviously abides by legal requirements, while incorporating flexible and 'informal' teaching and learning approaches.

The comments associated with learning are hardly surprising. It was school, but not school; school is partly meant to be about learning so it was learning but it wasn't learning, we had lessons, but not normal lessons, we learnt in lessons, but not in a recognizable way, or perhaps not things like maths because we did not do maths lessons. They were teachers, but not like most teachers, you are meant to learn from teachers, but they weren't like normal teachers, and so on.

This account must seem very familiar to many teachers. Attempts to introduce non-conventional ways of teaching and learning, have to face pupils' (and teachers' as well as Education Ministers') deeply-rooted notions as to what constitutes a recognizable learning experience. The search for clues in history lessons is viewed as not 'proper' history by some; cross-curricular approaches can be challenged in primary or secondary schools because there is no lesson labelled maths or geography; personal and social education work may be active and enjoyable, but for some observers and participants group work is not what they associated with recognizably legitimate learning; for many pupils, it is precisely the activity of writing and being stuck at a desk which they associate with the business of learning.

The evaluator's words might easily be translated into the words which many of the pupils were using. 'Serious' becomes, for example, 'boring' and learning in school is boring, so if school wasn't boring perhaps they were not learning; 'disciplined' could become 'strictness' and if the teachers were not strict, perhaps the pupils were not learning; 'structured' might become 'subjects' or the usual pattern to the school day, and if you are not doing subjects, or your time is not ordered according to the school bell, then perhaps you are not learning. Among other things, we seem to return here to convictions that if an experience is enjoyable, then it cannot really be a learning experience, a position which the advocates of play as learning continue to battle against in the early years of schooling and which the structured play report (Chapter 2) illustrates.

There is an irony then to such attempts to change the learning environment. In bringing about this change, it becomes difficult for many of the pupils to recognize the setting as one in which legitimate, proper, learning can take place. The pupils are, of course, not the only ones who have this difficulty, they share with others, including those at the pinnacle of educational decision making in this country, a strong body of taken-for-granted knowledge concerning what can count as recognizably legitimate learning activities within schools. We do, however, have resources now for whole curriculum planning which can both meet statutory requirements *and* provide a motivating and engaging experience for pupils. The pupils' views represented here certainly suggest the need to draw strongly on, for example the experience of TVEI extension, and to look at the curriculum reports in this book, for ways of changing schools appropriately for the twenty-first century. Jason would welcome that!

Concluding Comments

The previous chapters have illustrated a number of ways in which schools have been changing. The reports from teachers provide some sense of curriculum experiences which challenge our common sense knowledge about school life, about teachers and about pupils learning. The immediate challenge is to ensure that such approaches are taken into account as schools implement the National Curriculum.

There is certainly no disagreement here with the Education Reform Act in its requirement of schools that they must offer a curriculum which is:

balanced and broadly based. This curriculum must aim to: a) promote the spiritual, moral, cultural, mental and physical development of pupils at the school and of society, and b) prepare pupils for the opportunities, responsibilities and experiences of adult life.

(DES, 1988: p. 1)

We also note that the National Curriculum *From Policy to Practice* document (DES, 1989) was clear that 'the foundation subjects are certainly not a complete curriculum', and that the Education Reform Act 'does not require teaching to be provided under the foundation subject headings. Indeed, it deliberately allows flexibility for schools to provide their teaching in a variety of ways'.

There is, however, one crucial issue here which the curriculum reports point to again and again. This is to do with the entitlement of all pupils to effective and engaging learning experiences. One possible consequence of the National Curriculum is that many of the approaches illustrated in the reports might be increasingly restricted to very small target groups of disaffected and less able children. In addition, as the education system itself becomes more differentiated, including open enrolment, so some schools might attempt to make such pupils 'invisible' to their local communities and clients. There might be a reluctance in some schools to establish much in the way of the curricular provision outlined in this book. It is our strong belief that we need to fight for the retention and expansion of the learning experiences documented in the teachers' reports. It is also the view of the contributors that such experiences should not be viewed as only appropriate for certain 'types' of pupils, a sort of 'practical curriculum for practical kids'.

This position is equivalent to the old argument that personal and social education programmes are only necessary for certain 'types' of children (Hustler and Ashman, 1986). By contrast, the view we hold is that elements of the approaches in this book are necessary for all our pupils, that they are entitled to such experiences. This, then, is one of the central messages of the book and it is connected with a major worry. The worry is about the need for time if people are to take advantage of 'flexibility'. Just as the individual teacher needs to be above all else a 'reflective practitioner', someone who finds time to think about what is and is not working within the classroom, so time is needed to reflect on how best to implement overall curricular provision in schools. The worry is that the speed of educational change, in particular implementation of the National Curriculum and its associated testing programme, may lead to uncreative responses: responses which do not recognize ways in which certain kinds of learning experiences can be built in. Such a response will establish a return to a complete diet of 'normal lessons' in 'normal schools' and a schooling system which employers, parents, and pupils recognized was inflexible and outdated in the 1970s, let alone the 1990s.

If the above is the key issue raised by this book, many other concerns have been raised through the teachers' reports and some of these have not been addressed explicitly. We have not addressed the curriculum reports in relation to resource issues. To address this in detail, and omit other concerns, would have been misplaced on at least two counts. To begin with, the tremendous current changes for the management and resourcing of schools would rapidly date many of the arguments which could be put at this point. More importantly, perhaps, our general argument is that if schools feel that the approaches outlined in this book are of importance, then the resources will be found. Increasingly, it will be individual schools which will have the decision-making power here, it will be teachers, parents, governors and others who will need to be convinced. We also recognize that many of the curriculum reports raise equal opportunities concerns, particularly relating to gender, which deserve more attention than they have received here.

We hope that the reports will provide ideas and possibilities for teachers and for those entering the profession. We believe that these reports can be viewed as a form of evidence, at least as important as the language of some cruder 'performance indicators'. The reports display, for example, how schools can address the issue of cross-curricular themes, skills and dimensions. What will change will be the way the curriculum content of the activity is 'accounted for'. Two things are therefore important: that the experience of those staff with skills in managing these activities is recognized and made more widely available, and that the activities become more accountable, at least in part, in National Curriculum terms.

In fact, it is the very structure provided by the requirements of the National Curriculum, together with delegated school management, that will enable many schools to construct and implement school development plans looking forwards, rather than backwards to a 'normal schooling' of the nineteenth century. Some schools will, of course, unfortunately reproduce a schooling more appropriate to the Victorian era. It is the contention of the editors that in such schools 'normal school' will continue to be something which fails most of our pupils and from which they will seek to escape.

The curriculum reports are also a form of evidence in a different sense. They return us to points made in the introductory chapter concerning the capacities of teachers, capacities which are often ignored. We must make it more apparent to those outside schools that teachers cannot be viewed simply as delivery people for a curriculum package. A pupil's curriculum experience is finally shaped not by legislation but by how teachers and pupils work together. The curriculum reports document the enthusiasm and concern that teachers can bring to that task. Every pupil, including those of modest attainment and those who struggle to achieve even the lower levels of curriculum prescription, has an entitlement to a full curriculum experience and to be enabled to participate as fully as possible. This means that the kinds of detailed imaginative work developed in the reports in this book must be incorporated into school life.

We know that there are large numbers of teachers and other educationalists with a commitment to the principles and approaches outlined and discussed in previous chapters. There is a determination to continue to think through these ideas and to refine them. We have only just begun to really think about such approaches on a large scale and our education system must provide us all with time and space to consider what part they should play in a 'normal school' appropriate to the year 2000. We may begin to feel that a television broadcast showing a Minister for Education doing sums on a blackboard is not quite in tune with the times, though it may be in tune with our own memories of 'normal lessons'.

Bibliography

Barnes, D. (1976), *From Communication to Curriculum* (London: Penguin).

Barton, L. and Walker, S. (eds) (1986), *Youth, Unemployment and Schooling* (Milton Keynes: Open University).

Black, P.J. (1988), *Task Group on Assessment and Testing Report* (London: DES).

Britton, J. (1970), *Language and Learning* (London: Penguin).

Broadfoot, P.M. (1988), 'The National assessment framework and records of achievement' in H. Torrance, (ed.) *National Assessment and Testing: A Research Response* (Edinburgh: British Educational Research Association pp. 3–14).

Burgess, R.G. (1983), *Experiencing Comprehensive Education* (London: Methuen).

Carr, W. and Kemmis, S. (1986), *Becoming Critical: Education, Knowledge and Action Research* (London: Falmer).

Cockett, M. (1986), 'The Alternative Curriculum Strategies Project' in Hustler *et al.*, op.cit.

Cortis, G. (1977), *The Social Context of Teaching* (Wells: Open Books).

Cuff, E.C. and Payne, G. (eds) (1986), *Crisis in the Curriculum* (London: Croom Helm).

DES Inspectorate (1977), *Ten Good Schools* (London: HMSO).

DES (1988), *Education Reform Act, 1988* (London: HMSO).

DES (1989), *From Policy to Practice* section 4.13 (London: HMSO).

Evans, J. and Davies, B. (1986), 'Problems of Change, Teaching and Control' in E.C. Cuff and G. Payne, op.cit., pp. 106–137.

Galton, M., Simon, B. and Croll, P. (1980), *Inside the Primary Classroom* (London: Routledge and Kegan Paul).

Hammersley, M. and Woods, P. (eds) (1984), *Life in School* (Milton Keynes: Open University Press).

Hargreaves, D. (1984), *Improving Schools* (London: ILEA).

Hargreaves, D., *et al.* (1989), *Planning for School Development* (London: DES).

Holbrook, D. (1964), *The Secret Places* (London: Methuen).

Holt, J. (1971), *How Children Learn* (London: Pelican).

Holly, P. (1987), *The Dilemmas of Low Attainment* (London: Further Education Unit).

Hustler, D. (1988), 'It's not like normal lessons . . . you don't have to wag school any more' in A. Pollard, J. Purvis and G. Walford, op.cit., pp. 71–89.

Hustler, D. and Ashman, I. (1986), 'Personal and Social Education for all; Apart or Together?' in E.C. Cuff and G. Payne, op.cit., pp. 53–68.

Hustler, D., Cassidy, A. and Cuff, E.C. (eds) (1986), *Action Research in Classrooms and Schools* (London: Allen and Unwin).

Leech, N. and Wooster, A. (1986), *Personal and Social Skills* (Exeter: Religious and Moral Education Press).

Light, P. and Glachan, N. (1985), 'Facilitation of individual problem-solving through peer group interaction' in *Educational Psychologist*, Vol. 5, Nos. 3 and 4, pp. 217–26.

McNiff, J. (1988), *Action Research: Principles and Practice* (London: Macmillan).

Manning and Sharp (1977), *Structuring Play in the Early Years at School* (London: Ward Lock).

Mortimore, P. *et al.* (1988), *School Matters: The Junior Years* (Wells: Open Books).

Pollard, A., Purvis, J. and Walford, G. (1988), *Education, Training and the New Vocationalism* (Milton Keynes: Open University Press).

Rothery, A. (ed) (1984), *Children Reading Mathematics* (London: Murray).

Rutter, M. *et al.* (1979), *No Better Way to Teaching Writing* (Stroud: Thimble Press).

Turnbill, J. (1988), *Towards a Reading-Writing Classroom* (Portsmouth: Heinemann).

Weston, P. (1988), *The Search for Success* (Slough: National Foundation for Educational Research).

Woods, P. (1976), 'Having a laugh: an antidote to teaching' in M. Hammersley and P. Woods (eds) *The Process of Schooling* (London: Routledge and Kegan Paul).

Index

Printed in the United States
by Baker & Taylor Publisher Services